BETWEEN BARGAINING AND POLITICS

BETWEEN BARGAINING AND POLITICS

An Introduction to European Labor Relations

HANS SLOMP

Westport, Connecticut
London

Library of Congress Cataloging-in-Publication Data

Slomp, Hans, 1945–
      Between bargaining and politics : an introduction to European
labor relations / Hans Slomp.
          p.   cm.
      Includes bibliographical references and index.
      ISBN 0–275–95608–3 (alk. paper)—ISBN 0–275–96466–3 (pbk.)
      1. Trade-unions—Europe—Political activity.   2. Collective
bargaining—Europe.   3. Industrial relations—Europe   4. Post-
communism—Europe.   I. Title.
      HD6658.5.S59   1996
      322′2′094—dc20   96–2205

British Library Cataloguing in Publication Data is available.

Library of Congress Catalog Card Number: 96–2205
ISBN: 0–275–96466–3 (pbk.)

First published in 1996

Praeger Publishers, 88 Post Road West, Westport, CT 06881
An imprint of Greenwood Publishing Group, Inc.

Printed in the United States of America

The paper used in this book complies with the
Permanent Paper Standard issued by the National
Information Standards Organization (Z39.48–1984).

10 9 8 7 6 5 4 3 2 1

Contents

Acknowledgments ix

Introduction xi

1 Corporatism 1
  Tripartism 1
  Corporatism 3
  Preconditions for corporatism 5
  Types of corporatism 7
  Tripartism and peak-level talks in the larger countries 9

2 Trade Unions, Employers, Parties and Politics 13
  Craft unions and the British model 13
  Industrial unions on the continent 15
  Union-party relations 18
  Employers' associations 22
  Unions, employers and politics 25

3 A Short History 31
  1848-1880: Industrialization and craft unionism 31
  1890-1910: The emergence of social democracy 33
  1917-1920: The rise of communism 38
  1930-1950: Crisis, war and reconstruction 39
  1960-1974: The golden sixties 41
  Central Europe under communism 42

4 Labor Relations and Politics in the 1990s 45
  Technology and the labor market 45

The economy and the government 50
The end of dictatorship and the demise of communism
 in Latin Europe 53
New labor relations in Central Europe 55
New issues and new politics 57

5 Collective Bargaining and Conflict 63
Preconditions for sector bargaining 63
Collective bargaining and conflict in the British model 65
Collective bargaining and conflict in Germanic Europe 66
Collective bargaining and conflict in Latin Europe 69
National bargaining 72
Statutory wage policies 73
The public sector 75

6 Worker Participation in the Enterprise 79
A short history 79
Works councils 80
Trade union representation within the enterprise 83
Union representation and works councils in Germanic Europe 85
Union representation and works councils in Latin Europe 87
Co-determination 89

7 From Sector Uniformity to Enterprise Diversity 91
The Swedish Model: The example of the 1960s and 1970s 91
The German Model: The example of the 1980s and 1990s 93
The rise of the local union 96
The decentralization of collective bargaining 97
Employee participation in the 1990s 100

8 Labor Conditions in Europe 103
Wages 103
Working time 107
From health and safety to work environment 109
Social security and the European welfare state 110
Employment and employment protection 112

9 The European Union 115
A short history 115
Trade unions and employers 118
The EU impact on labor conditions 120
European works councils 123
Convergence or divergence? 125

10 Five Pairs of Nations   127
    Denmark and Norway   127
    Belgium and Holland   130
    Austria and Switzerland   132
    Portugal and Spain   135
    Hungary and Poland   137

11 A Summary in American Terms   141
    Labor relations and politics   141
    Employer-union contacts   144
    Worker participation   146
    The European welfare state   147

Bibliography   149

Index   161

Acknowledgments

A large part of this book was written as a text for the course "Labor Relations in the Smaller Nations of Europe" (ILRIC 337), which I taught at the New York State School of Industrial and Labor Relations of Cornell University during the spring semester of 1994. I am grateful to the Fulbright Commission for the generous Fulbright grant and to my home university for the leave of absence, which allowed me and my family to stay in the United States for seven months. This period, starting with more snow than we (and most Americans) had ever seen before and ending after travelling through Death Valley in July, will always remain a highlight of our lives.

A number of colleagues in the United States and in Europe have commented on earlier drafts or separate chapters. First, I am grateful to all twenty-five participants in my course at Cornell for gladly accepting the chapters that were completed as one of the texts for their course, for their many questions and suggestions, and for improving my English. I hope they enjoyed the course as much as I did. I also thank Roy Adams, Ton Bertrand, Dorette Corbey, Judit Czugler, Jacques van Hoof, Elena Iankova, Harry Katz, Peter Katzenstein, Ank Michels, Hans Moerel, Paul Nobelen, Jonas Pontusson, Max Rood, Joris van Ruysseveldt and Lowell Turner for their comments on earlier versions of the text or parts of it. My special thanks to Professor John P. Windmuller for kindly letting me use his office and for his many well-argued and critical remarks, to Won-Duck Lee for our discussions and walks and to Alison Cable of Cornell's International Office for her help and for our morning chat while I used her office.

Chapter 6 is a revised version of "National variations in worker participation," written for the Dutch Open University course on Human Resource Management. That text has been published in Anne-Wil Harzing and Joris Van Ruysseveldt (eds.) (1995) *International Human Resource Management: An Integrated*

Approach. London: Sage, 291-317. Parts of the book have also been used for the report "European Labor Relations: Supranational Models and National Systems of Labor Relations," written for the Korea Labor Institute, Seoul. Before the completion of the final manuscript a Polish translation was published by Ibidem, Lódź. Stanislawa Borkowska and Boguslawa Urbaniak suggested a number of changes in the Polish text which I have also adopted in the final version.

Introduction

Most Europeans tend to think in terms of national models of politics, culture and social life, except when they are in the United States and gladly overstep national boundaries to meet fellow Europeans. This "nationalist" attitude also permeates most surveys of European labor relations and politics, many of which are organized by country rather than cross-country.

This short introduction to European labor relations is an effort to provide a general Europe-wide view. Its only claim to originality is its Europe-wide focus, not just for one subject but for a whole range of developments in European labor relations. It is an attempt to transcend "nationalism" in labor relations by focusing on the continent as a whole and on groups of countries. The national focus is to some extent given up, not for a concentration on differences within nations but in favor of a discussion of common European developments.

As the survey in the following chapters shows, European labor relations have a few basic features in common, not only in collective bargaining and conflict but also in worker participation and in the role of the national governments. Looking at these common elements, the nature of European labor relations might be summarized as follows.

First, collective bargaining is practiced primarily by employers' associations and trade unions for each industrial and commercial sector at a time. On both sides the negotiations are coordinated to some extent by the all-industry confederations. Company bargaining is also common, but on the union side it is carried out within the framework of the organizations' policy for the sector as a whole and under the leadership of sector union officials. Most larger labor disputes take place during the annual period of bargaining and are called by the trade unions rather than by individual workers or the union representation within the enterprise. During the term of the agreement the unions generally refrain from calling strikes.

Second, a distinction is made in Europe between company bargaining and worker participation in enterprise decision making. Bargaining covers primary labor conditions like wages and total working time. Worker participation relates to the elaboration of the sector agreement for the company, to working conditions within the enterprise and to the broad outlines of the company's social policy. In larger companies the enterprise economic policy is also a subject of worker participation, in particular if it affects the level of employment. The trade unions monitor the process of worker participation and attempt to establish some conformity with their own policies, even if they do not dominate the works councils engaged in participation. Worker participation is practiced without overt conflict, and the unions actively commit workers to "peaceful" worker participation.

Third, the national governments are involved in labor relations in a number of ways. They provide a legal framework for bargaining, conflict and worker participation. They regulate labor conditions by law and closely monitor wage bargaining. Either sporadically or more often, they interfere in the bargaining process or in the resulting agreement if they deem the expected outcome detrimental to the national economy, particularly in times of high inflation and unemployment. Moreover, they act as employers in the public sector and sometimes use this position to influence the nature of labor relations and the negotiations in the private sector. On the other hand, the national unions and employers' confederations enjoy a special status as consultants to the national government and administrative agencies in the field of social and economic policies. Their voice is also heard in politics, due to the close ties between the organizations and political parties, in particular between the major unions and the social democratic and (former) communist parties.

In short, European labor relations is a three-party and a three-level affair. The three parties are the national employers' confederations and their member associations, the national trade union confederations and their member unions, and the national government. The three levels consist of the all-industry or national level, the industrial and commercial sectors or branches, and the individual enterprise. Different organizations meet at distinct levels. For instance, the national government is only minimally involved in branch- and enterprise-level labor relations (Slomp 1992).

The Continent-wide view offered here is a hazardous affair, of course. Talking about labor relations in, for instance, the Belgian steel industry or in British banking is a generalization and often implies a simplification. Speaking about national systems of labor relations simplifies even more, and discussing Europe as a whole may easily lead to oversimplification.

Indeed, a closer look at European collective bargaining, worker participation and government involvement discloses a wide range of national (and sectoral and regional) variations. Sector bargaining is especially cherished in Germany, with its tradition of sector agreements (*Tarife*), and in other northern European countries. At the opposite end of the continuum is Great Britain, where enterprise and shop floor bargaining prevail. The limitation of labor conflicts to the period of bargaining and to actions organized by the unions is also most pronounced in northern Europe. The other side is again represented by Britain and also by Italy with its frequent enterprise-level strikes.

The distinction between collective bargaining and worker participation is applied most rigorously where the two activities take place at different levels, that is, in northern Europe, including Germany. In that part of Europe the unions are also most actively engaged in committing their members to the no-strike pledge during the term of labor agreements, irrespective of the issues involved in the process of worker participation. The distinction is less clear in France and Italy, but Great Britain is the only country in which the distinction is hardly made and in which "normal" bargaining and worker participation overlap.

The role of the national government as an autonomous force in labor relations is strongest in France and southern European countries. They are used to a tradition of state stimulation (and especially in France also legal codification) of new social practice. In the smaller European nations the government is often half-hidden behind the veil of national-level talks, in which the employers' organizations and the unions assume responsibility for social and economic policies and sometimes also for wage policies. The link between labor relations and national politics is also strongest in France and southern Europe, with their large public sectors, the intimate ties between the national government and private large enterprise and the love-hate relationship between the unions and national governments, depending on the latter's composition and social performance. Government restraint is more prevalent in Britain and Germany. Even on this point the two countries differ considerably, however, because of the German government's active role as a legislator in labor relations versus the British tradition of "voluntarism," with far less legal sanctions.

To do justice to this diversity within Europe, without giving up the cross-national European view, a distinction is made between three models of labor relations. First, there is the British model, which also applies to Ireland--that is, to the "British Isles"--and which is the oldest type of labor relations. Second, there is the model which prevails in Germany and the smaller nations of northern and western Europe. Since all of them speak Germanic or "Teutonic" languages, minorities excepted, they will be called the Germanic nations. The group consists of Germany, Scandinavia (Denmark, Norway and Sweden), the Low Countries (Belgium and Holland) and the Alpine Countries (Austria and Switzerland). Third, is the model of labor relations which is typical of France and southern Europe. These nations speak Romanic languages, minorities excepted, and are often grouped together as "Latin Europe," a tradition that will be followed here. Latin Europe refers to France, the Iberian Peninsula (Portugal and Spain) and Italy.

This division applies to what is commonly called "Western Europe," that is the countries with a free market economy (and in most cases also a democratic political system) since World War II or longer. Within Western Europe the division is an obvious one and also one which is "felt" and appreciated by most Europeans as a cultural divide, separating the northerners from the southerners and the British from the continentals. This divide is due not so much to different types of people, as prejudice has it, but to historical differences in social structure and political processes. It has a strong impact on labor relations and politics, of course. The following chapters will reveal a variety of ways in which this influence is felt, against the background of showing a European pattern of labor relations.

The three groups are highly unequal in the number of nations and the number of people involved. The Germanic group contains more countries than the other groups put together, but in population size it is surpassed by the Latin group. It will become clear that the Scandinavian countries to some extent occupy a position of their own within the Germanic group but because of the many common features they share with the rest of the group they have not been set apart.

A few small Western European countries with less than half a million inhabitants (Iceland, Luxembourg and Malta) are excluded. Two other countries, Finland and Greece, occupy a special position, both in language (neither Germanic nor Romanic) and in labor relations and politics. Because of the links and increasing similarities with its Scandinavian neighbours, Finland has been classified as part of the Germanic group. For corresponding reasons Greece is counted among the Latin countries. However, both countries occupy a rather marginal position within these groups, and for that reason they are hardly referred to in the survey.

This classification into three groups does not include Central Europe, the countries that were under Soviet-Russian domination until the end of the 1980s (most of them speaking Slavonic languages). These nations are discussed more incidentally. This uneven treatment reflects the early stage of transition in which Central Europe still finds itself. The emergence of organizations and of mutual contacts between them and with the government is so new a phenomenon that it is very difficult to indicate general trends. The discussion of Central Europe mainly focuses on Bulgaria, Czechia, Hungary and Poland. The other countries of Central Europe, including the former Yugoslavia, are excluded from this work, if only because of a general lack of information. This also applies to Eastern Europe, the nations which formed part of the Soviet Union.

To summarize the geographical terms used:

The British Isles:	· Great Britain
	· Ireland
Germanic Europe:	· Germany
	· Scandinavia (Denmark, Norway, Sweden)
	· the Low Countries (Belgium, Holland)
	· the Alpine Countries (Austria, Switzerland)
	· Finland (which is not a Germanic language country)

Latin Europe:	• France
	• Italy
	• the Iberian Peninsula (Portugal, Spain)
	• Greece (which is not a Latin language country)
Central Europe	• the text refers only to Bulgaria, Czechia, Hungary, and Poland

Throughout the text, the term "continent" is used for Western Europe, that is, the combination of Germanic and Latin Europe. Only if stated explicitly does it also refer to Central Europe.

This book combines the focus on the general structure and practice of European labor relations with short historical notes and discussion of ongoing trends. It is made up of three parts. In accordance with the prominent place of the national government in European labor relations, chapters 1 through 4 discuss the link between labor relations and politics, starting with what may be called the European invention par excellence--corporatism. The second Chapter offers a more general discussion of the links between the labor relations organizations and national politics. Chapter 3 gives a very short history, going back to the roots of present day European labor relations, and it highlights a few decisive periods in labor relations history. The last chapter in this part discusses recent developments.

The second part of the book covers labor relations in a stricter sense. It consists of Chapters 5 through 7. Chapter 5 focuses on the contacts between trade unions and employers' organizations in the form of bargaining and conflict, while Chapter 6 centers on worker participation within the enterprise. The last chapter in this part is devoted to recent trends.

The third part consists of three chapters without a common focus. Chapter 8 contains a survey of current labor conditions in Europe. Chapter 9 is devoted to the impact of the European Union on labor relations. Chapter 10 compares five pairs of smaller nations, whose national peculiarities are less known. This chapter should compensate somewhat for the bird's eye view in the rest of the book. Discussing pairs of comparable nations has the advantage of showing subtle differences and national variations within the larger context of the other chapters. The exclusive concentration on smaller nations in this chapter seems justified because the four nations of Western Europe with over fifty million inhabitants (France, Germany, Great Britain, and Italy) are referred to in most of the chapters in a comparative perspective. Separate discussion would overlap with the extensive coverage in the rest of the text. Moreover, it is in the relative differences among small countries belonging to the same Germanic or Latin group that the subtleties of European labor relations can best be demonstrated.

The last chapter summarizes European labor relations using American terminology. Its purpose is not to provide a comparison of American and European labor relations but a short application of American terms to the subject of this book, in order to foster a better understanding of European labor relations among non-Europeans.

References in the text and the bibliography are mainly confined to comparative literature and, for practical reasons, to literature in English. The bibliography includes a few compilations of nation studies as a key to further reading on specific nations.

1

Corporatism

Arguably the most distinctive feature of European labor relations is the meetings between trade unions, employers' associations and national governments. These contacts form an integral part of national politics in a number of countries. The agreements (or the lack of agreement) resulting from the late afternoon or evening sessions never fail to make the front page of the national papers the next morning. Such "tripartite" contacts have become a major research interest since the mid-1970s.

TRIPARTISM

What is tripartism? Tripartism consists of regular contacts between the peak organizations of trade unions and employers--that is, those at the national confederation or federation level--and the national government in order to discuss issues of social and economic concern, like labor legislation, taxation and social security, employment policies and industrial policy. The subjects covered may extend to other fields, including public education, health care and housing provisions. In some countries special tripartite councils have been established for these contacts. The most prominent one is the Dutch Social and Economic Council (*Sociaal-Economische Raad*, SER), housed in a large office in the government seat. It consists of eleven trade union representatives, eleven employers' association leaders, and an additional eleven independent outside experts, including the presidents of the National Bank and the National Planning Office. A number of specialized committees, which also involve trade union and employer representatives and outside experts (mostly university professors), prepare the plenary discussions. Belgium possesses two such councils, one for social and one for economic affairs, both with fewer outside experts than in the

Dutch SER. However, in Belgium more pressing issues are discussed at peak-level talks outside the councils. In Scandinavia, tripartism is a more informal affair, consisting of regular meetings, held up to once a week, between government ministers and the leaders of the trade union and employers' confederations, without academic experts or an office of its own. In cases where government-union-employer contacts take place sporadically, rather than on a regular basis, the term tripartism is not used. Instead, we speak of peak-level talks.

Two aspects have generally been regarded as basic to tripartism: the limitation of the talks to a few peak organizations, which are able to speak on behalf of their members, and the involvement of these organizations in the formation of state policies. First, tripartism can function only where the number of participants is limited. Thus, only a few organizations, recognized as the official representatives of segments of the population, are able to express their demands or their views in tripartite talks. Their selection provides them with a monopoly position and affords them extra status and influence in national politics. Other organizations may be refused this status. The main argument for this refusal is that these other organizations are not "representative," being either too small or having too narrow an interest, such as one professional group or one category of employees. Or they may be considered too radical by the national government or the other selected organizations, and as potential disturbers of the talks. In practice, the arguments of size, coverage and attitudes are also used as a mere pretext for the organizations involved in tripartism to keep others out, since any newcomers reduce the power of the other participants. In Scandinavia this has not been a major problem, since one organization has been dominant on both the union and the employer side. In the Low Countries, the labor movement is divided and new organizations have sprung up, arousing discussion about their admission.

Related to the representational monopoly of one or a few organizations is the fact that tripartite talks only make sense when the organizations involved are able to speak on behalf of their members and to conclude agreements which their members will adhere to. The organizations must be capable of enforcing compliance with the results of the talks. That does not exclude democratic decision-making procedures within the organizations, but once an agreement is concluded the members of the organizations must live up to it. Thus, tripartism requires the existence of representative organizations, that can speak on behalf of large numbers of people and of strong organizations able to commit their members.

The second aspect of tripartism is the involvement of the participating organizations in the formation, and sometimes also in the implementation, of state policies. The talks are useful to the national government only if there is a chance of winning the support of the organizations. Tripartism has an important function in national politics. It legitimizes the government's policies by giving them a stamp of approval from the organizations which are directly affected. An additional advantage for the national government is that this involvement takes the policies out of the political sphere by shifting part of the responsibility to the organizations affected. This shift constitutes a "de-politicization" of government policy, because it takes some of the responsibility for social and economic policy making out of the political sphere (the national government, responsible to the parliament), and moves it towards the sphere of labor relations, for which the national government does not bear direct responsibility. Those who oppose the measures can no longer direct their arrows against the government but rather to the organizations involved. This is not just an advantage for the government. The shift from politics to labor relations through policy involvement of large organizations reduces the number of claims made to the government and in so doing contributes to the stability of the political system. De-politicization prevents the "overload" of that system with all kinds of claims from social groups and organizations which might endanger its stability (Lehmbruch 1977). Tripartism may also be used to take the sting out of a hot political issue, by having union and employer experts study the matter for some time; essentially the matter is mothballed until emotions have calmed down.

For the organizations involved, tripartism offers influence over state policies without any "official" responsibility. Their support is dependent upon the opportunities the government provides them to influence state policies. And in case something goes wrong, the organizations can always lay blame on the government, even if they consented to the measures proposed, by saying that they had no other choice or were outvoted. This shows that tripartism requires some degree of mutual understanding. If employers, unions and the national government shift the responsibility too often, tripartism will end.

One of the major subjects of tripartite talks has been wage policy. The confederations are able to influence social and economic policy, but at the same time they, particularly the unions, must either monitor sector bargaining or permit the national government to do so. This combination of wage restraint and influence over social and economic policy has even been called a "trade-off" or "exchange," because the influence compensated the wage moderation. Although these terms overstate the case, since they imply that wage policies are as important as all other forms of social policy combined, they rightly point to the close link between tripartism and wage coordination. However, the degree of wage coordination and government intervention varies considerably in countries with traditions of tripartism (Lange 1984; Castles 1987b).

CORPORATISM

Schmitter (1974) drew international attention to the importance of tripartite contacts in European labor relations and politics and coined the term "neo-corporatism." The word was derived from the term "corporatism," used at the end of the nineteenth century by the Catholic Church to denote the cooperation between unions and employers' associations at the level of the industrial branch or the economic sector, as well as at the national level, that aimed at a kind of self-rule by employers and unions. It implied a representational monopoly for one or a few organizations to take care of social and economic policies for the sector involved, and on a more encompassing scale for the whole nation. The Catholic Church advocated this sector and national corporatism (so called because it involved "corporations" of workers and employers) as an alternative to a strong state or to an unbridled class war between workers and employers. In the 1920s and the 1930s corporatism took on a negative connotation when fascist dictators, in imitation of Mussolini's Italy, imposed this kind of cooperation after first dissolving the unions that were not willing to participate. Although this fascist "state corporatism" was influenced by the Catholic ideal, it was not a device used to prevent a powerful state, as corporatism had been in the Catholic doctrine; rather, it was an instrument of the state, used to impose its order.

Thus, the concept of corporatism has referred to different forms of employer-union-government contacts (Cox and O'Sullivan 1988). In the Catholic doctrine it denoted union-employer cooperation to prevent a strong state. Under fascism it meant state-enforced cooperation between employers and state-monitored unions. In recent times it has referred to common efforts by unions, employers' associations and the national government to shape national policies. Schmitter recognized these differences, but he pointed to the representational monopoly they had in common: Some organizations are allowed to participate, others are not. Hence "neo-corporatism" and "democratic corporatism" are the terms under which tripartite contacts have become a major topic in labor relations literature. In this text we will use the shorter term corporatism instead of neo-corporatism or democratic corporatism.

The terms tripartism and corporatism are sometimes used without distinction, but corporatism is mostly used in a wider context that includes not only tripartism, but also the type of labor relations that are characterized by tripartism and by a kind of social partnership between trade unions, employers and the national government--that is, for systems in which tripartism has a strong social base in the relationship among the organizations involved. This culture of social partnership is basic to corporatism, providing a solid base for continuous peak-level contacts which "mere" tripartism lacks. As a consequence, corporatism is more stable than tripartism. The latter requires a certain degree of mutual understanding, not a more lasting partnership between unions, employers' associations and the national government. This union-employer-government partnership constitutes the third feature of corporatism, in addition to the monopoly of representation and the organizations' involvement in public policy (Schmitter and Lehmbruch 1979; Lehmbruch and Schmitter 1982).

Schmitter's emphasis on the negative side of corporatism, the monopoly of one or a few organizations, was motivated by the comparison with its opposite--pluralism. Pluralism refers to a situation in which groups and organizations compete for a willing ear from the national government, but in which the national government ultimately decides to whom it will listen without giving up any responsibility for its policies. This "open market" for influence appears to be more democratic, since it is the government or the elected parliament which decides on policies. However, those favoring corporatism point out that corporatism also allows employers and unions to compete for influence, and that even when they agree the government is under no obligation to follow their advice. Moreover, others are not hindered from voicing their opinion, although they have to do so outside the tripartite talks. And corporatism does not pose a threat to the government's responsibility to parliament--a core element in European liberal democracy--since the parliament can always overrule the agreement reached in tripartite talks.

Corporatism eventually became regarded as a positive term, largely because the countries in which it was strongest seemed to fare better after the 1974 oil crisis. They showed signs of a national consensus to weather the crisis and to retain or improve their world market position, in particular by common efforts to restrain wage increases. Thus, corporatism became the slogan for a crisis-resistant system of labor relations--a strategy for survival to be introduced at will, and all European democracies were rated on scales of corporatism. France mostly ranked at the bottom of the list, Austria and Sweden at the top (Pekkarinen, Pohjola, and Rowthorn 1991).

PRECONDITIONS FOR CORPORATISM

The differences in degree of corporatism lead to the question of why some nations rank higher and why others are less fortunate. Three explanations have been offered, referring to economics, to the labor relations organizations and to national politics. The economic explanation, offered by Katzenstein, stresses the fact that corporatism has been confined to the smaller European nations: Scandinavia, the Low Countries, and the Alpine Countries. Despite the economic obstacles these countries face, because they are too small to influence the functioning of the international economy yet are compelled to follow its cycles, they occupy a strong position in the world market. They have specialized in specific industrial production, serving protected niches in the world market. In combination with this specialization, they have developed an ideology of partnership and even of national consensus in order to survive (Katzenstein 1985).

The second explanation, stressed by a number of authors (including Schmitter 1974 and Therborn 1991), points to the existence of well-organized trade unions and employers' associations that have developed a bargaining relationship in the course of the twentieth century and are able and willing to enforce the results of the negotiations upon their members. Both organized and unorganized workers, as well as individual employers, have to comply with the bargaining outcome--at least most of the time.

The political explanation, which is also mentioned by several authors, suggests the existence of a link between the trade union confederations and political parties currently participating in government or with a fair chance of participation in the next government (Cameron 1984). Because of the importance of wage policy as an issue in corporatist talks, the trade unions, even more than the employers' organizations, should have a good relationship with the national government.

In combination, the three explanations treat corporatism as a northern European small-nation phenomenon developed in Scandinavia (later joined by Finland), the Low Countries and the Alpine Countries. Only these countries meet the economic, organizational and political requirements stressed in each of the explanations. All of them are small in terms of population size; with the exception of Holland (fifteen million), they have between four and ten million inhabitants each. In these countries strong trade unions developed at the turn of the century that were linked to social democratic or Catholic parties. Corporatism actually developed in the 1930s or 1940s when the economic crisis and later the devastation of Europe made all groups launch a common call for national reconstruction in close cooperation. Invariably, it started at a time of social democratic participation in government, a condition that predisposed the social democratic unions to engage in talks and to discuss social measures. Moreover, it encouraged employers to participate in talks with the trade unions in order to limit the national government's role in labor relations. Once corporatism had been firmly established, it continued under governments without social democrats.

In Scandinavia, corporatism started with a union-employer agreement. Examples are the Norwegian 1935 Basic Agreement (*Hovedaftale*) and the 1938 Saltsjöbaden Agreement in Sweden. (Denmark had been the first country with such a Basic Agreement, concluded in 1899!) Both agreements combined a declaration of intent to solve labor disputes without recourse to overt conflict with procedures to be followed in case of disputes. The Basic Agreements have served as a kind of two-party "constitution" of labor relations between the "labor market parties," as unions and employers' associations are called in Scandinavia. The national governments came in later, without reducing the role of the peak-level contacts between the two parties.

In contrast, peak-level talks in the Low Countries were a three-party affair from the very beginning, also involving politicians. In Belgium, tripartism started with a peak-level meeting in 1936 after a nationwide strike movement. The foundation for postwar developments in Belgium was laid by a "Social Pact," discussed during the wartime occupation by union leaders, prominent employers and politicians. The pact covered postwar wage measures, institutions of union-employer cooperation and a system of social security. The existence of Catholic unions in the Low Countries was less conducive to the rise of tripartism than the presence of social democratic unions, since the Catholic unions were smaller than the social democratic ones and were only a minor partner within the Catholic parties--in addition to the Catholic middle class, employers and farmers organizations.

TYPES OF CORPORATISM

The varying starting conditions led to the existence of different types of corporatism, that is, to a further differentiation within the group of small nations. One clear difference exists between corporatism that had its roots in a union-employer agreement, and a second form in which the government played a very active role from the beginning. The Scandinavian countries, and Sweden most of all, are examples of the first type. Corporatism was founded on basic agreements concluded by the umbrella organizations of trade unions and employers. These agreements have been regularly renewed and extended to cover new fields, including worker participation and environmental issues. The role of the national government was rather limited from the outset. It was merely accepted as a third partner because the other two parties wanted to ensure government approval of their plans or because they expected concessions from the government--in tax policy, for example. This limited role of government has had substantial effects on labor legislation. Since the trade unions and the employers' federations have been able to settle a number of issues among themselves, they did not need any legal backing on these points. As a consequence, labor legislation covers fewer subjects in Scandinavia than in the rest of Europe.

The opposite is the case in Holland. Dutch corporatism has been government-initiated and government-steered and laid down in extensive and elaborate labor legislation. The prominent role of the national government was related to the division of the unions and employers' associations along religious (both Catholic and Protestant) and other lines, linked to political parties which were represented in government. Belgium and Austria fall between these extremes. In Belgium informal talks have always been just as or even more important than formal institutions. Legislation and two-party agreements have intermingled, but such agreements are almost always sanctioned by law. In Austria corporatism is officially a voluntary two-party affair, embodied in a Joint Committee (*Paritätische Kommission*). It is embedded in an extensive legal framework, however, and government ministers play a prominent role. This difference in the position of the national government, and in the need for labor legislation, is related to a second distinction--between corporatism based on consensus and corporatism based on conflict.

Corporatism is generally considered as an expression of consensus. Unions, employers' organizations and the national government cooperate on the basis of common interests, with some measure of similar objectives in mind. Korpi defended an opposite view in a history of the Swedish welfare state. To him the welfare state is an accomplishment of the Swedish social democrats. It was reached without much overt conflict, because the social democrats--that is, the combination of the party in power for most of the time since the 1930s and a very strong trade union movement--did not need such conflicts. Their power impressed other groups, including employers, to such an extent that they were able to enforce most of their objectives in a process of bargaining and legislation rather than in overt conflict (Korpi 1983). This argument treats the Swedish (or Scandinavian) system as a form of "institutionalized" conflict, in which the basic conflict between trade unions and employers permeates all elements of society, including the bargaining process between the peak organizations and the consultation of the peak organizations by the national government.

Korpi probably overstated the case. If corporatism had been based on the employers' fear of the strong social democratic movement, it would certainly have shown more tensions in its forty-year history. Korpi's stress on conflict is useful, however, because it highlights differences in interest, rather than the common interests between employers and trade unions. By doing so, it points to different bases of corporatism. In Scandinavia, and in Sweden most of all, the social democratic movement is a very strong one. Social democrats dominate the government and there are large social democratic trade unions without rival movements. They have been able to enforce cooperation on the basis of their strength. In the Low Countries the social democratic movement is not as powerful, since it traditionally has had to compete with a Catholic labor movement, and in Holland also with a Protestant one. In both countries the national governments have played a role in bringing about union-employer cooperation. The difference in force leads to differences in institutional structures: more employer-union autonomy in Sweden, more government steering in the Low Countries, with Austria in between. Institutions count, but so does the relative strength of the forces that have shaped them.

Katzenstein makes a distinction between two types of corporatism, liberal and social corporatism, also taking into account differences in labor's strength. The liberal corporatist states (the Low Countries and Switzerland) display a more offensive, employer-oriented strategy in the world market, for which they rely on their private sector industries and services. In the social corporatist countries (Denmark, Norway and Austria) a strong labor movement is able to enforce a different and more defensive strategy of adaptation to the world market, based on a larger public sector and a lower export intensity. Sweden is a combination of both types. While in liberal corporatism employers and conservatives have been able to dictate their terms upon a weak labor movement, in social corporatism they have given in to a strong labor movement (Katzenstein 1985).

Three types of corporatism have been distinguished here:

- union-employer based versus government-steered corporatism;
- corporatism based on labor's strength versus corporatism based on a weak labor movement;
- social versus liberal corporatism.

The lines of distinction overlap to some extent. The first type mentioned (union-employer based, labor strength-based, social) is more at home in Scandinavia and the second (government-steered, based on weak labor, liberal) in the Low Countries, but several variations exist. The partial overlap leads to the conclusion that the strength of the labor movement has a large impact on the type of corporatism that exists.

TRIPARTISM AND PEAK-LEVEL TALKS IN THE LARGER COUNTRIES

The group of corporatist countries does not include any of the larger nations--Germany, Great Britain, France, and Italy, each with over fifty million inhabitants. In addition to their stronger position in the world market, partly due to their larger home market, the larger countries differ from the corporatist countries in the other preconditions for corporatism--the organizational structure of trade unions and employers' associations and the union-government relationship.

In organizational structure Germany is closest to the corporatist countries. The only general peak organization is the German Trade Union Confederation (*Deutsche Gewerkschaftsbund*, DGB). It coordinates a small number of well-organized unions, which are the real centers of power in German labor relations. The DGB's lack of power over the member unions is a major difference with the power structure in the corporatist countries.

Great Britain is more distinct from the corporatist nations than is Germany. Its trade union confederation, the Trade Union Congress (TUC) also enjoys a monopoly, but its position towards the member unions is weaker than the DGB's. This has to do with the decentralization of British trade unionism, with a large number of autonomous unions and a high premium put on membership initiative. The resulting diversity is not considered a weakness of the system, as it would be in the corporatist countries or in Germany, but a democratic asset not to be lost by efforts to bring about more unity. Enforcing compliance with national agreements does not fit in with the appreciation of diversity.

In contrast to Germany and Great Britain, both France and Italy possess a number of trade union confederations which are highly competitive. They coordinate the member unions' activities and exercise some power over these unions. However, backing spontaneous action and extending it to larger protest movements is regarded as the core trade union activity. Since they cherish worker militancy, neither the confederations nor the member unions are willing to impose membership discipline to the degree that is done in the corporatist countries or by the DGB's member unions in Germany. Enforcing compliance with agreements would interfere with the spontaneity of worker protest. To some extent employers share this appreciation of individual initiative in labor relations, far more than their colleagues in the corporatist countries or Germany. Stated simplistically, German trade unions, like those in the corporatist countries, stress membership discipline, while the British unions stress membership initiative and the French and Italian unions membership militancy.

On the second point, the relationship between trade unions and political parties in government, Germany once again is closest to the corporatist countries. Although the DGB formally is an independent and neutral organization, strong informal ties connect it with the social democratic party. As in the corporatist countries, the two entities regard themselves as part of a wider labor movement, reinforcing each other's strengths and compensating for each other's weaknesses. A major difference with the corporatist nations has been the absence of the German social democrats from the national government during the postwar reconstruction period.

The ties between British trade unions and the British Labour Party are also close, although they are quite different from those in Germany. In accordance with the decentralization of British trade unionism, the link is one between the Labour Party and the many member unions of the TUC, rather than with the TUC as such.

The major French and Italian confederations have stressed their political independence, like the DGB, but they have long been linked to the communist party and dominated by communists. In contrast to social democratic parties and the British Labour Party, the communists have been almost permanently excluded from the national government in the second half of the twentieth century. They are represented in parliament, but at the same time stress the need of a political and social revolution, which would put an end to the existing political order. The major trade union confederations share this ideal, and their own role as a political opposition force. Tripartism does not fit that opposition role. The only kind of peak-level contacts acceptable to them have been meetings at which the national government is willing to comply with union demands or presses employers to bow to these demands.

As one might expect, central-level contacts in these four countries have been sporadic. In Germany, peak-level talks were held in the late 1960s, as an effort of "concerted action" (*Konzertierte Aktion*) with respect to economic policy and wage policy. It ended after a few years when it became clear to the unions that the major purpose of the government in pursuing this common action was wage restraint. In Great Britain the only example of a national agreement has been a "Social Contract" between the Labour Party and the TUC in the mid-1970s. The employers did not participate in these talks. The Contract aimed at preventing party-union conflict after a period of heavy conflicts between the unions and a Conservative government in the early 1970s. It offered the repeal of a number of Conservative Acts on trade union affairs and tax measures in exchange for wage moderation. Probably its main effect was to stimulate a short-lived discussion on the emergence of corporatism in Britain.

French and Italian peak level meetings are distinct from those in Great Britain and Germany. They were enforced by the unions during the heyday of spontaneously started workers' actions in order to get concessions from the government or the employers. Under pressure from the unions and the large waves of strikes, the national governments used to organize such meetings. Because of the concessions these governments offered or pressed the employers to offer, the unions could hail the meetings and their outcome as their own accomplishment, or in the rhetoric used, as "victories of the working class." Due to the size of the strike movements and the issues covered, two such series of meetings in France stand out as major landmarks in European labor history. They were the 1936 meetings resulting in the Accord Matignon and the 1968 meetings which led to the Constat de Grenelle.

The 1936 meetings were held in the Prime Minister's office, Hotel Matignon. They were called by a socialist government whose rise to power unleashed an enormous spontaneous strike wave. The new prime minister then summoned the employers to the bargaining table and pressed them to make a number of concessions. The Matignon agreement contained the employers' pledge to engage in collective bargaining, the recognition of the right to unionize and the recognition of workers' representatives within the enterprise. The government itself promised legislation to introduce the forty-hour work week and two weeks of paid holidays. This outcome formed a striking contrast with a similar sequence of events in Belgium, which directly followed the French events. A large spontaneous strike wave in that country, an imitation of the French one, prompted the government to call a National Labor Conference. That conference also met with fierce employer resistance, but it formed the beginning of a series of such conferences right before and after World War II and set in motion a development towards corporatism.

The 1968 Constat (Statement) de Grenelle, named after the Paris street where the Ministry of Labor is located and where the talks were held, was also the result of a large and spontaneously started strike wave, involving at its peak ten million workers. (It is still in the Guinness Book of Records as the largest strike movement ever, with over 150 million working days lost.) The sequence was similar to the one in 1936, and so were the concessions. They included the gradual introduction of the forty-hour work week, which had been lost after the war, and the recognition of union representatives within the enterprise, including legislation on that subject. Because the major union confederation, the General Confederation of Labor (*Confédération générale du travail*, CGT) refused to sign the agreement, it remained a mere statement (*constat*). In the thirty years between and in later years there have been less prominent peak-level meetings in France, but their number has been limited.

In Italy, peak-level meetings have been less rare than in France, but they have been concentrated within a few periods. The most outstanding one was the Hot Autumn (*autunno caldo*) of 1969, in which spontaneous strikes spread over the country. The union confederations encouraged and extended the strikes as a means of pressure for a number of reforms in social legislation, including housing, health care and social security. The unions also engaged in direct negotiations with the government in order to discuss their claims. In addition to these union-government talks, there have been three-party meetings. At times, Italy has even had periods of burgeoning tripartism. Due to the attitude of the communist-dominated union movement towards the national government and the lack of membership commitment, the development towards tripartism has not materialized, however. One of the outcomes of the *autonno caldo* was the 1970 Workers' Statute (*Statuto dei Lavoratori*). This document, a declaration of intent rather than a piece of legislation, promoted a number of individual workers' rights, such as employment protection, individual privacy and worker representation. The Italian statute served as an example for a comparable Spanish Workers' Statute (*Estatuto de los Trabajadores*) enacted in 1980, a few years after the fall of the fascist dictatorship in that country.

The short periods of German peak-level talks bear most resemblance to corporatism. Indeed, in the organizations' structure and in the union-party relationship, Germany is closer to the corporatist countries than any of the other larger countries. An important difference is the weak position of the union confederation DGB towards the member organizations.

In the following chapters there will be less focus on the confederate level. Rather, the focus will be on trade unions and employers' organizations in general, which will highlight the similarities between Germany and the corporatist countries. The differences in organizational structure--as well as union and employer relations with the national government--between the Germanic, the British, and the Latin systems of labor relations will be elaborated in the next chapter.

2

Trade Unions, Employers, Parties and Politics

At the end of the first chapter a distinction was suggested between three models of trade unionism, with different types of trade union organizations and union-state relations. This chapter discusses the three models in a more systematic way and extends them to models of labor relations, not just trade unionism. It also includes employers' associations in the discussion. Because the British type of trade unionism was the first to develop, and the other models were to some extent based on it, the British type is discussed first.

CRAFT UNIONS AND THE BRITISH MODEL

The difference between British trade unions and the other forms of trade unionism is not merely one of degree of decentralization. British trade unionism has retained an old type of organization, the craft union, which has almost disappeared on the continent. The best known example is the engineers union, one of the oldest European unions, which was founded in 1851. Traditionally, British trade unionism has been characterized by the predominance of such craft unions. They were established by skilled workers in a trade and excluded the unskilled or the less skilled in the same industry. This type of trade unionism has traditionally displayed the following activities or functions:

- The integration of workers within the craft tradition;
- The improvement of labor conditions by setting wage rates, either unilaterally by the unions or in contacts with employers, and by imposing checks upon the flow of unskilled newcomers and apprentices to the trade;
- The improvement of living conditions by providing social security benefits for workers unable to work, or their families.

The first activity includes discussion of technical and social developments which affect the trade and standards of craftsmanship for the skilled as well as for apprentices. The aim is to provide a forum for workers with similar interests in the trade based on common skills.

The second activity initially consisted of setting wage rates and trying to get these rates accepted by employers, or at least inducing employers to comply with the wage rates. In the course of time this unilateral decision making was replaced by collective bargaining with employers, either for the craft as a whole or within each enterprise separately. One of the means to enforce the wage rates has been to limit entry into the trade by fixing the number of apprentices to be trained by the skilled workers. This restriction prevents the erosion of the craft tradition by breaking up the skilled workers' responsibilities into a sequence of activities, each of which can be performed by less skilled workers. The dilution of skilled work has been a fundamental concern of craft unions, mainly because of its impact on the wage rates but also because of its effects on the first function--the integration of a selected group of workers in the craft tradition. Dilution not only affects the skilled workers involved in it, but also jeopardizes the craft as such. Another means to protect craft standards, prevent dilution and maintain specific labor conditions is the "closed shop." This amounts to the refusal to work with non-union members, thus forcing all workers in the same profession within an enterprise to be or become union members. Workers who do not comply with this obligation or with union rules and policies will be fired by the employer if necessary under pressure of a strike. The closed shop forces the employer to enforce union rules in return for union efforts to maintain craft standards in their work.

The third activity was a supplement to the second one. It prevented workers who lost their income from falling into poverty. The early organizations concentrating on the third function were called "friendly societies." Some of them functioned independently from trade unions, which then stressed the first two functions. In the nineteenth century, most trade unions combined the three types of activities. In the course of the twentieth century, the latter function has become less important because of state-provided social security.

Craft unions exclude the unskilled, and as a consequence, the latter have to organize in separate unions--the "general workers" unions. The first of these general workers unions date from the 1880s. Transport workers then admitted general workers from various industrial branches into their organization. This Transport and General Workers Union, TGWU, has long been the largest single trade union in Britain. Since the end of the nineteenth century British trade unionism has been a combination of a few large unions which also or mainly cover general workers and a large number of smaller craft unions. Already in that same century technical and economic developments affected the traditional crafts, undermining the position of the skilled worker. The craft unions often regarded such technical innovation as a threat to their position and as deliberate employer attacks upon the unions, while employers pointed to the need to meet the standards of international or national competition. The dilution of old skills, the rise of new production methods and the emergence of new industrial branches have not only been a source of constant union-employer dispute, but also of inter-union demarcation disputes. Due to the borderlines between skills and skill levels, such conflicts can easily arise. The TUC then mediates, but it lacks the authority to impose decisions, and as a consequence, such conflicts often linger on for some time. The amalgamation of unions has reduced these tensions. Since the 1970s the number of TUC members has been reduced from over several hundred to just over seventy (still a much higher number than in most continental countries) due to reorganizations and amalgamations. Until the recent German reunification, the TUC was the largest trade union confederation in Western Europe, the only one with over ten million members. Since then, the German DGB has taken over.

INDUSTRIAL UNIONS ON THE CONTINENT

British trade unionism forms a striking contrast with the trade union movement on the European continent. Craft unions formed one of the foundations of that movement, but they were abandoned when trade unions became part of a wider political movement, like social democracy in northern Europe or more radical labor movements in Latin Europe. Trade unionism on the continent has also displayed a number of functions:

- To integrate workers in a national (and international) political movement;
- To improve labor conditions by means of collective bargaining and political claims;
- To improve living conditions by means of social security benefits and by political claims.

The first function is basic to continental unions. Unions either make up or form part of a political movement, which has a far wider horizon than the working conditions of the union members. This movement claims to represent the whole working class, without any distinction between skill levels. Demarcation lines between trade unions are irrelevant for this political class movement or for the industrial struggle against employers. At first, craft demarcation lines were accepted, since the early unions were organized on that basis and some of them did not want to give up their exclusivity at once, if only because they had just started or passed the test, by surviving a lockout. Unskilled workers were then organized in "general workers" unions or "factory workers" unions, as in Great Britain. The ideal, however, was industrial unionism, with borderlines between industrial branches and sectors as the only line of division. In the course of the twentieth century industrial unionism became the accepted form of organization. Already before World War II most continental unions had reorganized along these lines. The number of member unions in the Belgian socialist confederation had been reduced to 24 by then, most of them industrial unions. At the same time some traditional craft unions continued to exist. The victory of industrial unionism was complete after World War II, when most unions had to make a fresh start. Germany did so most thoroughly. Only sixteen unions became affiliated with the DGB, but they covered all categories of workers. Other countries did the same. The major exception was Denmark where trade unionism developed very early and where the traditional craft and general workers remained intact--part of a wider social democratic movement as in the rest of the Germanic countries. Since industrial unions did not defend craft rules, concentrated on sector rather than enterprise activities and organized skilled as well as unskilled workers, they did not try to enforce the "closed shop" principle, or gave up such efforts early in their history. As a consequence the closed shop is an exception on the continent.

A general deviation from the rule of industrial unionism concerns clerical workers. When the political movement started at the turn of the century, there was a debate if clerical workers should be allowed to join as fellow workers, or should be excluded as middle-class agents. In most countries their small unions were admitted after some time, but neither they, nor the other unions wanted to extend the principle of industrial unionism to clerical workers, in view of their different positions within the enterprise. The German union reorganization of 1948 was path breaking in that it removed this line of demarcation and organized clerical workers in the industrial unions. In addition to the absence of other (religious) unions, this manual-clerical workers unity made the DGB claim it had achieved the ideal of "unified unionism" (*Einheitsgewerkschaft*): one social democratic organization for all workers, not divided along status or craft lines but organized on the basis of industrial branch or sector. Not all clerical workers in Germany were willing to give up their own unions for that ideal, and they established a separate clerical workers' confederation. Such separate confederations of clerical workers or even of middle and higher echelon staff exist in most European countries. In the Low Countries they have been major contestants for seats in the tripartite councils. Public sector workers have always been organized in separate organizations, but that results from the nature of their employer, the state or local authorities, not from status lines.

Industrial unionism has given rise to far fewer inter-union demarcation disputes than have craft unions. Such disputes may arise in the case of the emergence of new industrial branches, but they are easily solved under the confederation's pressure. An example was the rise of artificial fibers in the 1960s. Textile industry unions claimed this branch for themselves, but the chemical industry unions also wanted to organize the new branch.

The second and third functions of continental unions--the improvement of labor conditions and provision of social security benefits--have been similar to those of the traditional craft unions. They have been adapted to industrial unionism, however, and place a greater emphasis on political claims. As part of a political movement the unions themselves forwarded demands for labor legislation or supported the social democratic party's claims. The function of providing social security has been taken over by the state in most countries. Only in Belgium, Denmark and Sweden do the trade unions still play an active role in unemployment insurance with trade union unemployment funds, or as benefit-paying institutions for state-provided social security. This function is generally regarded as one of the major causes of the high unionization rate, over seventy percent, in these three countries.

The main organizational difference between the Germanic and Latin models is the centralization of decision making in the Germanic movements and the decentralization in the Latin model. In the former, the industrial unions are able to enforce discipline and compliance upon their members. No protest action, be it a strike or a political action, is started until the union leadership has decided to do so. Individual participation in the decision making prior to the decision is welcomed, but individual calls for action are not allowed. Individual action would only impair any organized and collective action. In the Latin labor movement, such private initiative is the very essence of trade unionism, which then mobilizes the other workers.

Moreover, in the Germanic model, the confederations have more power over the member unions than in the Latin unions. The "weakest" confederation in Germanic Europe is the German DGB, which sets it apart from the confederations in the corporatist countries. This relatively weak position was imposed after the end of World War II by the Allied Powers. They pressed all kinds of social organizations, including the unions, to decentralize in order to provide more room for democratic grassroots initiative. Decentralization also served to prevent an easy takeover of trade unionism and other organizations by fascists or communists, as had happened in 1933 when the Nazis seized power.

In general, the Latin union movements are also less well organized, with a smaller bureaucracy and a lower unionization rate. Union density in the Germanic group of countries ranges from just under thirty percent in Switzerland and Holland to over seventy percent in Denmark and Belgium and even to over eighty percent in Sweden. It is much lower in the Latin group, where it ranges from less than ten percent in France--the lowest rate in Europe--to almost thirty percent in Italy and Portugal, just above Switzerland and Holland, the two countries that tail the Germanic group. With over fifty percent, Great Britain's position would be somewhere in the middle of the Germanic group, above the German rate of over forty percent (Bean and Holden 1992).

However, there have been important changes in union density over time, which complicate the discussion on the causes and the effects of trade union density. Recently, Visser has contributed to the debate on economic and political influences on the unionization rate by scrutinizing all union membership data, taking into account the number of retired and other non-active workers who are union members. The new data even changed the debate on French unionism, since the unions in that country had always published highly inflated membership figures (Visser 1990).

In sum, the main distinction in trade unionism is one between Great Britain and the continent. In Britain, craft unions complemented by general workers' unions predominate. Ireland shares this combination, a legacy of British rule over that country. The craft and general workers' unions are highly autonomous and primarily look after the interests of their own members.

On the continent, craft unions have been replaced by industrial unions, which are part of a broader class movement, speaking for the whole working class. A major deviation from the principle of industrial unionism are clerical workers' unions. They defend specific interests and are often coordinated by separate confederations. The major confederations may also possess one or more clerical workers' unions, however. A more important line of division on the continent is along religious or ideological lines. In most Germanic nations one single social democratic oriented confederation enjoys a virtual monopoly. In the rest of the group (the Low Countries and Switzerland) Catholic unions exist beside the social democratic ones. The Belgian Catholic union confederation has even outgrown the social democratic one, and as a consequence this is the only country in which the Catholic trade union movement is the largest one. In Latin Europe communists predominate, with rival socialist movements. Only in Spain is the communist-dominated union movement second to the socialist one. This rivalry between unions is another reason for the virtual absence of the closed shop on the continent.

UNION-PARTY RELATIONS

The differences in union-party relations between the British unions and the social democrats and communists on the continent have been just as pronounced as those in the type of organizations. Only the British unions have established their own political party. They did so in the beginning of the twentieth century, after a long period of labor cooperation with the liberals, the so called "Lib-Lab" politics. A major motive to found the Labour Party was to put an end to governmental and judicial interference with labor relations to guarantee a free sphere of labor relations in which the unions could pursue their policies. It was not a political organization to serve the interests of the working class as a whole but an instrument of the unions, serving the highly differentiated union interests.

The TUC by itself is not affiliated with the Labour Party, but most member unions are. The British unions have financed the Labour Party by means of a political levy, which is part of the union dues. That political contribution has been much disputed. Some union members have regarded it as a deviation from the voluntarist nature of British unionism, since it forces union members to pay this levy. The response has been to open the possibility of "contracting out," a written declaration that one refuses to pay that part of the union dues. Conservative governments have also tried to do something about this compulsory levy by enforcing a change from "contracting out" to "contracting in." This means union dues may only be used for political purposes after an explicit declaration of consent by union members, which would supposedly make it easier for members to refuse the levy. In a Trade Union Act, passed in 1984, the Conservative government withdrew a clause to the effect of "contracting in," after union pledges of stricter guidelines for the unions' political funds.

The combination of union funds, bloc votes for the trade unions in the Labour Party and the fact that union leaders have been ministers in Labour governments sounds impressive. In practice, the union influence on the party has been limited. The unions have often been divided on major issues, Labour governments follow their own course, and the unions realize that too much of a union grip over the Party would deter non-union voters in the elections. Even more important is the union priority of enforcing social improvement by means of bargaining for their own members, instead of using political means.

In the Germanic model, a close yet different relationship exists between social democratic trade union confederations and the social democratic parties (Padgett and Paterson 1991). The unions have always regarded themselves as part of a broader political class movement. While they are the "industrial" arm of that movement, the party is the political arm. In combination, they try to enforce social improvement for the entire working class. Since the industrial and the political strategies have their own logic of action, the two may interchange, but they should not interfere with each other. In practice, this means that the unions take care of collective bargaining but do not engage in political strikes. Hence, a neat distinction is made between the political struggle, pursued by the party, and the industrial struggle, in the form of collective bargaining by the unions.

Since the end of World War II, the relationship has been informal rather than formal, a change aimed at attracting non-union voters to the party and, even more, non-party members to the unions. In Germany the formal separation between the DGB and the social democratic party was especially intended to prevent the revival of Catholic trade unions. Political levies and bloc votes are out of the question for the same reasons in the Germanic countries. Intimate links exist, however, at leadership level. Social democratic politicians, including cabinet ministers, have been recruited from the ranks of union officials, and union leaders have occupied seats in parliament. In practice, most social democratic parties reserve a number of such seats for prominent trade union leaders and try to recruit prominent union members for participation in party committees. The same applies to Catholic (and Protestant) union-party relations in the Low Countries and Switzerland. In the religious parties the union impact has always been smaller, due to the presence of other Catholic organizations (middle class, employers, farmers) without socialist counterparts.

The close ties at the leadership level were reduced in the early 1970s under pressure from the spontaneous actions and the opposition against hierarchical trade union structures. Since that time trade union leaders in the Low Countries have given up their seats in parliament, stressing union independence vis-à-vis the party in order to respond better to such spontaneous initiatives. However, the trade unions have remained one of the major pillars, if not the main base of the social democratic parties, and the step from a union career to one within the party is still a small one.

In the Latin model union-party relations have also been close, but again are different. Communists have long dominated the largest French confederation, the *Confédération générale du travail* (CGT), as well as the largest Italian confederation, the similarly named *Confederazione Generale Italiana del Lavoro* (CGIL). The same applies to the second largest Spanish and the largest Portuguese confederations since the fall of fascism in the 1970s. Even more than the social democratic unions, the communist-dominated union confederations have stressed their formal independence from the party, but the same close, informal ties at the leadership level have characterized both movements. Moreover, communist ideology has stressed the total predominance of the party over other political and social organizations and the union function as "transmission belts" of the communist party.

The term "transmission belt," coined by Lenin in the 1920s for the Russian unions after the 1917 communist revolution in that country, denotes a relationship in which the unions mainly serve to recruit members to the communist party, to enforce worker compliance with party decisions, and to transmit worker suggestions to the party. These functions have to be fulfilled in total union submission to the party. The term has also been used by outsiders for the communist-dominated union confederations in Latin Europe. It rightly points out that initiative for political action comes mostly from the party leadership and that party considerations have been overwhelming in the confederations' attitudes towards national governments. That makes the term useful for the party-union relationship. For other activities, including strikes and collective bargaining, it suggests far too much hierarchy and unity. There have been strong thrusts of anarchism and anarcho-syndicalism in these countries, advocating spontaneous action. They share the revolutionary aims of communism, but not its strict and hierarchical organization. While the communist cells are tightly knit and the communist party is well organized, the unions are much less so. The communists have organized themselves only in order better to mobilize others, without the need to permanently organize the less committed. This also in part explains the low unionization rate in Latin Europe. Workers join during a large strike, to leave again after some time or to linger on as non-paying members. Moreover, the term "transmission belt" also suggests too much ideological unity. In addition to communists and anarchists the communist-dominated union confederations have included reformist unions and several brands of socialism, with fierce debate among them about attitudes towards political parties.

Partly due to the predominance of communist unions, linked to communist parties which opposed almost all governments, political strikes have been frequent in Latin Europe. Communist calls for protest have been followed by strikes which are explicitly directed against the national government, and the unions have also been eager to extend spontaneous political protest. Such actions are not always protests against government policies. They may also be efforts to draw the national government into bargaining--thus serving as a means of pressure against employers. The national government is not only an enemy. Any government, whatever its composition, may also be changed into an ally by putting enough pressure upon it. It will then rally forces against employers and mandate them to the bargaining table. The French actions leading to the Accord Matignon in 1936 were of that type. The Italian strikes in 1968 and 1969 were both directed against the national government and against employers, as is generally the case in Italy and in Latin Europe. Hence, the Latin model does not make the neat distinction between industrial action, pursued by the unions, and political action by the political party. The two may often be combined, for instance when the government is called upon to interfere during a strike, and the strike then becomes a means to press the government.

In the Latin model there also exist trade union confederations which call themselves socialist and in some cases have links with the socialist parties. The term "social democratic" is rarely used in relation to these Latin parties and unions because it stresses too strongly strict organization and discipline rather than the ideas of spontaneous movement and ideological diversity. In the Germanic social democrats' view the Latin socialist parties and unions lack the mass base among workers, the commitment towards parliamentary politics, and the strong organization required for those purposes. Indeed, socialist parties in Latin Europe have often been confined to intellectuals and specific groups like teachers and clerical workers in the public sector. Only in Spain has the socialist union confederation surpassed the communist-dominated one and has the socialist party become a lasting force with a large and stable following among manual workers. Greece is rather exceptional, because the major Greek confederation is a socialist one, but in its subordination to the socialist party it is more comparable to the communist unions.

Despite the intimate links between unions and politics, the differences between the three models are very pronounced. In Britain the unions until recently exercised some influence in the Labour Party by means of their bloc votes, but their main priority is outside the realm of politics. In the Germanic countries the unions are heavily represented in all kinds of party bodies, but they do not dominate the party and they enjoy total autonomy from the party. In the Latin countries the communist trade unions have been dominated by the communist party and have at times served as an instrument of the party's political action.

The three models share the combination of rank-and-file union and party activities. Almost all party activists in the social democratic, socialist, and communist parties, as well as workers active in the Catholic parties, are also active trade union members, and many union activists are also active party members. Trade unions in Europe are ideologically committed movements, even if they are formally independent from political parties. Joining a trade union is as much an act of political commitment as it is a step to support collective bargaining. It is more an act of solidarity than simply a means to secure personal gains. Of course, the unions are concerned about "free riders" who enjoy the advantages wrought by trade unions without being union members. This problem is discussed in the unions, but it does not trouble most union members. Not being a union member is considered more an expression of a general lack of political and social solidarity than a rational choice to obtain something for nothing. In particular American literature tends to stress the nature of unions as organizations joined for personal benefits. The classic theory in this respect has been offered by Olson, who stressed the personal benefits and the free-rider problem. He also made a fine distinction between large organizations, with more social responsibility, and smaller organizations, mainly aiming at material advantages for their members (Olson 1965). Europeans do not lack self-interest, of course, but in joining a European trade union more than personal gain is involved (Hartley 1992).

EMPLOYERS' ASSOCIATIONS

The structure of employers' organizations also differs among the three models (Windmuller and Gladstone 1984). Actually, industrialists had established associations before the rise of trade unions, but these organizations were adapted, or new associations created to face the unions and act as employers' organizations. Because most employers' organizations have less of an organizational structure than trade unions, they are often called employers' associations rather than employers' organizations.

Great Britain has the same diversity in employers' associations as in trade unionism. The Confederation of British Industry (CBI) has a very large number of member associations, most of which organize only a minority of the eligible enterprises. The Germanic countries have stronger confederations with smaller numbers of member associations (though often more than the number of unions) and a higher organization rate, up to ninety percent. In terms of power over the member associations the German Federal Confederation of German Employers' Associations (*Bundesvereinigung deutscher Arbeitgeberverbände,* BDA) is the weakest organization in Germanic Europe, like the DGB on the union side. In general, the Latin employers' associations are weaker than the Germanic ones. They enjoy a much higher organization rate than the Latin unions, however, and they are less plagued by ideological split. In both respects the difference between the Latin and the Germanic employers' associations is smaller than between the Latin and the Germanic trade unions. The French confederation is called General Council of French employers (*Conseil national du patronat francais,* CNPF), and the Italian one is called Confindustria. Most of the European employers' confederations combine political activities, in contacts with the national government, with social activities, in contacts with the trade unions. In the corporatist countries of the Germanic group, this combination of activities is partly carried on in tripartite talks and councils.

Although employers' associations lack the ideological or religious split of the union movement (only in Holland have Catholic and Protestant organizations long been active participants in bargaining beside the major confederation), there have been a few lines of separation. First, in some countries there exist separate associations for contacts with the trade unions and (sometimes older) associations advocating the employers' economic interests. The most prominent example of this division of labor is Germany, where an industrialists' confederation (the BDI) exists beside the BDA. A second line of division is between industry and commercial services. Where separate umbrella organizations exist, the industrial confederation is often the larger and the leading one, represented in national talks and councils. A third division is one of enterprise size. In many countries smaller enterprises have their own organizations, which they can join in addition to the general confederation. The small enterprises' associations often remain in the shadow of the general confederations, however, and the latter will also speak for them in peak-level contacts.

These lines of division are common throughout Europe. There are only a few countries with one peak association which represents all interests at the same time (social and political, industry and services, as well as small enterprises). However, since the 1960s several mergers have reduced the number of peak organizations, causing a general trend towards one general employers' confederation.

Publicly owned companies belong to these employer associations or remain unorganized. The large Italian public sector has an association of its own, Intersind, which plays an important role in that country's labor relations, rivaling the position of the private sector's Confindustria. In public services there often exist state-sponsored agencies which act as employers' associations for national and local government workers and employees of state-financed enterprises.

The link between employers' association and national politics has always been less close than the one between unions and politics. In contrast to workers, employers have only rarely set up their own political parties. They vote for parties on the political right (conservatives, liberals) or center right (Christian Democrats, liberals), which also draw support from the middle classes of small shopkeepers, professionals and clerical workers, and often also rural interests. Indeed, unlike social democracy or communism, no single political party can be called an employers' party, and in most countries the political right has been divided more than the political left. In particular, Castles has drawn attention to the division of the political right, rather than characteristics of the labor movement, to explain labor's success (Castles 1987a). Probably the major cleavage has been the one between the middle class of small shopkeepers and other small entrepreneurs, and the owners and managers of large industry, the industrial elite--with the former more often supporting Christian Democracy and the latter liberal or conservative parties.

Employers' associations have often kept a low political profile since as organizations they could easily be seen by their own members as possible intruders upon free enterprise, and political involvement might reinforce that impression. However, Christian Democratic parties have always stressed the need for a strong employer representation in their ranks in order to counterbalance or even outweigh the Christian Democratic trade unions. Another reason for the low political profile was that the many lines of division might be possible causes of discord. While the unions were mainly set up to take care of the workers' social interests, the early employers' associations often started as clubs discussing the members' economic interests. The shift or extension of their scope to social affairs was a source of friction in itself. To some extent the lines of division are related to the nature of the enterprise, like the one between large and small enterprises. But there also exist lines of regional diversity between sectors and industrial branches, between industry and services, and between export-oriented sectors and protected industries.

This low level of political involvement by employers' associations has left ample room for individual employers to become active in politics, something workers could not afford except as paid representatives of the labor movement. Indeed, while workers are almost completely dependent upon their organization to express their political interests, since they are hardly able to do so as individuals, employers can voice their wishes individually. They do not need their associations, but derive authority from their position as employers. Employers who occupy political functions are rather rare, however. The burdensome process of democratic decision making, involving clashes between ideologies and long talks about the detailed wording of state measures, does not appeal to them. Many of them feel a certain contempt for politicians who need so much time to arrive at decisions and when they do make a decision never keep their word. The employers who are politically active often also play a prominent role in the employers' associations, though they stress their independence.

There have been differences between the three models. In Great Britain employers share the Conservative Party with the rest of the middle class and the landed estates. On the continent the political right is divided. The Scandinavian political right consists of liberal and conservative parties, sometimes called the "bourgeois bloc," despite that it has seldom displayed unity. Since World War II these parties have been in power only in periods with long intervals between them. In the other Germanic countries, Christian Democrats and liberals compete for middle class and employers' votes. During most of the postwar period the Christian Democrats have been the only party in government or the largest coalition party, governing in combination with the liberals or the social democrats.

In Latin Europe, the political right is just as divided, but the parties involved have been in power most of the time because communists and socialists refused to cooperate with each other--and even combined would not reach a majority position most of the time. Christian Democrats have been a very prominent force in politics only in Italy--until their recent downfall. In France and the Iberian

Peninsula there have been a number of conservative or liberal parties, united only in their anti-communism stance. In France, General De Gaulle tried to put an end to the frequent deadlocks in French politics by founding the Fifth French Republic in 1958. He became the core and later the hero of the large conservative Gaullist party, which has not been able, however, to attain a monopoly at the right of the political spectrum.

Fascism also has often been discussed as a middle class movement, attracting small entrepreneurs. Indeed, most fascist movements, as well as German Nazism, appealed to the middle class, with their appreciation of traditional authority, the family, order and discipline, and their condemnation of international capitalism. The appeal has been small in Britain and most of the smaller Germanic countries, where the middle class was integrated in political parties that participated in or even monopolized government until World War II. In Latin Europe the predominantly Catholic middle-class employers more easily supported fascism as a counterforce against the radical and anti-Catholic attitude of the labor movement. All Latin countries have had periods of fascist or reactionary rightist rule--Italy from the early 1920s until 1943, the Iberian Peninsula from the 1930s to the 1970s, France during World War II. German Nazism is a specific case for which specific conditions applied, like the country's international position and the longer history of imperial rule. Some of these conditions also drew German large industry towards Nazism. One of the elements conducive to its rise and to its expansion among the middle class, may have been the middle-class fear of being caught between the highly organized and large labor movement on the one hand and the steel magnates like Krupp and other very large companies on the other.

UNIONS, EMPLOYERS AND POLITICS

The models of labor relations show different forms of union and employer representation in politics. In Great Britain the two have their "own" parties, and conservatives and labor have alternated in government, with longer periods of conservative rule. In the Germanic models two variations exist. In Scandinavia politics has been labor-dominated. Social democrats have participated as the major party in national government, even monopolizing government most of the time since World War II. During a number of years the political right outnumbered the social democrats, but its division kept it from assuming power. In most other Germanic countries national politics has hardly ever been labor-dominated, but it has been partly labor-oriented and partly employer-oriented, due to the Christian Democratic domination of national politics. Since the Christian Democrats have formed coalitions with liberal, conservative and social democratic parties, the orientation towards labor has varied over time. In Latin Europe the government orientation favored employers most of the time until the 1980s. Labor-based parties were too small or too divided to form a majority. Moreover, the rightist parties have always been determined to keep the large communist parties out of government.

The impact of the political differences on social policy will be discussed in Chapter 8. Here, the focus is on the importance of politics--and of state legislation in particular--for labor relations and labor conditions. Or, stated otherwise, does politics matter in labor relations?

In Great Britain labor relations and legislation are less closely linked than on the continent. The unions, and many employers as well, regard most labor legislation as attempts to interfere with their own activities. To overstate their belief, the best labor legislation is no labor legislation. Of course, there are examples of laws supported by the unions, but most government attempts to introduce labor legislation have met with overt union hostility. Hence, in Britain the unions draw a very sharp line between labor conditions and living conditions. The former are the unions' own field of activity, and neither the Conservative Party nor the Labour Party should interfere with it. Living conditions are the subject of politics, in which the unions will not interfere except by means of their influence in the Labour Party. In accordance, there have hardly been any political strikes in Britain, apart from strikes in the public sector. The only major political strike, until a series of long-lasting miners' strikes broke out in the 1970s and 1980s to fight mine closures, was the 1926 Great Strike, over wage reductions in coal mining.

In the Germanic model the line of demarcation between union and party activities is less strict. As in Great Britain, social legislation to improve living conditions is a party affair, except for union unemployment funds in some countries. In contrast to Britain, labor conditions are not simply the unions' (and employers') domain, to be respected by the national government. Rather, labor conditions are primarily handled by unions in contacts with employers, with the government offering a helping hand. Compared to bargaining, legislation is of secondary importance, however. The primacy of bargaining--that is, of the industrial over the political strategy--implies that collective bargaining should not be jeopardized by regular calls for state intervention unless this takes place with the consent of both parties involved. The distinction between bargaining and political strategy, and the priority of the former, makes the position of the national government one of relative neutrality towards employers and unions. As an institution above the parties or on the sideline, it is relatively uncontested, which facilitates the business of government and leads to political stability.

One of the main objectives of labor legislation is to extend bargaining results to non-organized employers or to apply a generally approved minimum with respect to specific working conditions (or a maximum for work hours).   Labor legislation, then, is often based upon what is already practiced in a number of enterprises or industrial sectors. It constitutes less of a breakthrough than a sanctioning of existing practice, and because of this social base it is generally complied with. Unions and employers' associations are interested in generalizing bargaining results and in checking whether they are complied with. Examples of this kind of legislation are laws with respect to collective bargaining and conflict, which are based on current practice. Legislation on working time follows the same rule. It sanctions the workday or the work week that is already in force in a number of sectors or enterprises. Scandinavia comes closest to Britain in this respect, since the parties prefer to deal with labor relations themselves, without state legislation, at least most of the time. Corporatism supported by legislation is the "ultimate" form of bargaining supported by legislation, since unions and employers negotiate labor conditions as well as social legislation. In accordance with the primacy of bargaining, political strikes have been just as exceptional in the Germanic countries as in Britain, with only one or two such strikes in each country during the last fifty years, excluding public sector strikes.

At times, legislation may be used to enforce a breakthrough, for example during a long stalemate in union-employer relations. In the second half of the twentieth century unions sometimes shifted from an industrial to a more political strategy, particularly when they were under pressure from their members for more drastic action and sympathetic (social democratic) parties dominated the national government or participated in it. The latter by itself is not enough, since a union shift towards politics would affect both the union-employer bargaining relationship and put at risk the relatively undisputed position of the national government. Social democratic governments are not willing to jeopardize their position by a major clash with one of the parties unless there are very serious reasons to do so. A major example of this shift from bargaining towards politics occurred in the 1970s, under pressure from the wave of militancy which started in May 1968. Economic recessions periodically favor such a shift because the unions are looking for some redress and for gains they are not able to obtain in bargaining at times of unemployment. In such cases, however, the degree of worker militancy is at its low tide, which makes it easier for governments to turn down union demands. This has happened in the 1980s and 1990s under pressure from deficits in state budgets and the ideological reappraisal of the free market.

A specific subject in which national legislation has more often forced innovation is worker participation within an enterprise. Its specific nature as a non-consensual and contested issue is due to the fact that it does not easily lend itself to a compromise, like wages or working hours. It is not a question of more or less, but one of "either-or." Moreover, this is an issue in which employers' associations tend to be divided, which makes them less willing to add to internal discord by concluding agreements with the unions.

The fact that most labor legislation in the Germanic model is based upon social practice--interrupted only by a few contested breakthroughs, in particular in worker participation--reduces the impact of politics on labor relations. For living conditions, such as health care, housing, and education national politics may, of course, play a preponderant role. This combination of strong trade unions engaged in bargaining and a strong related political party active in social politics rather than in labor legislation is often called the "social democratic complex" or "social democratic model," exemplified in particular by Scandinavia and Austria. These countries are only more pronounced variants, with a strong labor movement, of the pattern of labor legislation that is to be found in all Germanic countries (Esping-Andersen and Korpi 1984). The crucial element is not so much whether there exists extensive labor legislation or not, but rather whether it is based on current practice and some degree of union-employer agreement. In combination with the organizational strength of the parties involved, the basis of legislation is decisive for the rate of compliance with labor laws, that is, for their impact. In contrast to Scandinavia, labor relations in Germany are very strictly ruled by legal provision, but most of it rests on common agreement or extends current practice, with worker participation as a prominent exception. The need for legal backing is greater when unions and employers' associations are weaker in terms of coverage and division.

In the Latin model bargaining has developed less over time. This makes for a different relationship between bargaining and labor legislation. First, legislation, and state measures in general, are used as an alternative to bargaining. Due to strained union-employer relations and the predominance of political struggle, the unions regularly attempt to forge a breakthrough in labor conditions with a large strike, aimed at government intervention. For that reason Latin unions call political strikes or turn "normal" strikes into political actions. In all Latin countries, large nationwide political strikes are considered to be the high spots of worker militancy and working class politics. Conservative governments occasionally give in. Moreover, the rare governments dominated by the political left are able to implement reforms right after they come to power, since they don't have to wait until unions and employers have reached an agreement. In neither case does labor legislation enjoy the employers' approval, which adds to the labor movement's joy over this new victory of the working class. However, employers are opposed to it and will, if they are unable to turn the tide, evade the legislation as much as possible. In particular in France the result consists of "*grands projets*" of legislation, which introduce new trends rather than sanction ongoing developments but which are hardly lived up to. Examples are the 1936 Accord Matignon and the 1968 Constat de Grenelle, whose legal outcome met with fierce employer resistance and overt employer sabotage. Italian entrepreneurs have shared this "opportunistic" attitude towards state measures (Italian governments make less use of of formal legislation), complying if conditions require but ignoring compliance under more favorable conditions.

A second type of state measure in the Latin group consists of government attempts to stimulate collective bargaining and a de-politicization of labor relations, which would make the government's position less contested and more similar to the one in the Germanic model. However, both unions and employers are eager to disdain such legislation, since it would be helping the enemy and supporting the other side's cause. Therefore, neither of them will comply. Hence, although almost each piece of legislation or other state measure in the Latin model constitutes a real breakthrough in labor relations and labor conditions and is often more innovative than legislation in the Germanic model, its effect will be reduced by the limited amount of compliance. Politics matter more than in

Germanic Europe, but the effect is the same or less. In particular France has seen various attempts at promoting bargaining by means of legislation, but any new laws seem only to reduce the chances of compliance, since they are regarded by both parties as another example of state intervention hailed by the unions and detested by the *patrons*, or vice versa. To the Latin unions, then, there is less of a separation between labor conditions and living conditions. Both are to be improved primarily by means of state action, interspersed with periods of bargaining.

3

A Short History

How did the differences in the three models of labor relations come about? The variation is due to a number of important developments in twentieth century European history, including the two world wars (1914-18 and 1939-45), but its roots go back to the nineteenth century.

The rise of craft unions took place after 1850. On the continent, their development was hampered by anti-union state policies. There, the labor movement became a political one, with industrial rather than craft unions attracting skilled as well as less skilled workers. In Germanic Europe the unions were related to social democratic parties. In Latin Europe communism became a major trend after World War I and a dominant movement after World War II. By that time the smaller Germanic nations had developed corporatism, in response to the crisis and to the war (based on Slomp 1990; see also Crouch 1993; Adams 1995).

1848-1880: INDUSTRIALIZATION AND CRAFT UNIONISM

By the mid-nineteenth century Great Britain was the only industrialized country and the leading power in Europe. Industrial sectors contributing to the industrialization were cotton mills, steel works, machine building and mining. In the textile mills there was only a small proportion of skilled workers, with a larger proportion in the steel works and engineering. In addition to these sectors, skilled workers were found in the growing building and printing industries and in the docks of the larger ports. Skilled workers also abounded in traditional crafts like shoemaking and tailoring. Unskilled male workers were employed in railway construction and mining; female workers, all of them unskilled, worked in the textile mills.

After a series of failed attempts by other skilled workers, the engineers were the first to organize a lasting national trade union in 1851. It survived a large lockout and was able to force its wage rates upon the employers. Other skilled trades followed this example, and when they were unable to dictate their wage rates, they engaged in collective bargaining with employers in order to fix uniform wage rates. Besides wage rates, a second motive to set up trade unions was to limit the number of apprentices admitted to the trade, a strategy which would also help to keep wages up. Many unions served as "friendly societies," providing social benefits to the members in case of illness and old age. Employers' associations emerged in a number of sectors, often in response to the rise of trade unions. One of their main activities was to fight the unions by means of lockouts, in order to defend the employer prerogative in setting wage rates. Slowly, however, collective bargaining came to supplant more contentious forms of contact between the unions and the employers' associations.

The British government hardly interfered in these organizational efforts and in the employer-union contacts. The unions incidentally lobbied for specific legislation--for example to reduce competition by low paid women--but political campaigning remained a minor activity. In 1868 the unions and local "trade union councils," which coordinated local union activities, founded the TUC, to discuss common issues, such as voting rights for the members and the response to lockouts. At first it was no more than an annual congress and was not provided with power over the member unions. In politics, the unions cooperated with the Liberal Party, the so-called "Lib-Lab" cooperation.

The European continent allowed less room for trade unionism. A few countries were industrializing in this period, but almost everywhere industry was concentrated in a few dispersed regions while the traditional crafts were concentrated in the national capitals. In some countries traditional journeymen's organizations were still alive. The 1789 French revolution had attempted to put an end to these organizations, since they were seen as an obstacle to individual freedom, equality and brotherhood (*liberté, égalité, fraternité*). In other countries authoritarian rulers banned such organizations as a potential threat to the established political order.

The 1848 street revolts and revolutions were the first international expression of worker discontent. They especially affected large continental capitals like Paris, Berlin and Vienna. Craft and skilled workers from various trades joined hands in these political protest movements. The revolution made the ruling classes, including the aristocracy and the urban bourgeoisie, as well as absolute monarchs, aware of the danger the working class posed to the established hierarchy. Workers constituted a "dangerous class," and all efforts at organization among them were to be suppressed. In spite of the ban, craft workers and printers were able to set up trade unions.

An upsurge of liberalism in the course of the 1860s--stressing free trade, the freedom to set up organizations and the right to strike--made a number of nations lift the ban on trade unions. The ruling classes hoped for a development towards non-revolutionary and relatively apolitical trade unionism, an imitation of the British example. Indeed, Great Britain was the example for most craft workers' organizations on the continent, in particular after the start of the "First International" in 1862, which was a combination of craft unions and political organizations. German unions, to some extent following the British example, influenced the rest of the continent. In the same period political movements sprang up with a revolutionary socialist ideology. They hailed the 1871 Paris Commune as a precursor to the socialist revolution. However, the main effect of the Commune was to reinforce the idea that workers constituted a "dangerous class" and to split the "First International." The increased international suppression of workers organizations after the Commune affected the German unions most of all. The 1878 Socialists Law (*Sozialistengesetz*) outlawed the socialist unions but not the Social Democratic Workers Party (*Sozialdemokratische Arbeiterpartei*, SDAP), which had been founded in 1869. Employers' associations had not yet emerged on the continent. Industrialists had their local clubs and trade associations, but they dealt with international trade tariffs and other economic questions, not with labor conditions.

As 1880 neared, only Britain possessed a number of unions in a range of industries, a nationwide and loosely organized coordinating union body (TUC) and a few employers' associations. On the continent the legal or illegal workers movement consisted of a few political organizations and a small number of craft unions, in particular in the printing industry.

1890-1910: THE EMERGENCE OF SOCIAL DEMOCRACY

Mining, the steel industry, railway construction and textile mills constituted the core sectors of the continental industrialization drive at the end of the nineteenth century. The combination of industrialization and urbanization made the construction industry an important economic sector as well. By the beginning of the new century, industrial towns had multiplied and new towns had sprung up, connected by national railroad networks. The most prominent example of this urbanization was the Ruhr area, the largest industrial region in Europe. New sectors, employing many skilled workers, included the electrotechnical industry and the first automobile works. Female industrial labor was still predominantly contained in the large textile mills, but the major source of work for women outside agriculture consisted of household services for the bourgeoisie and the growing urban middle class.

In this period the three parts of Europe showed different processes of "working class formation," including the ways in which labor expressed discontent and organized for action (Katznelson and Zolberg 1986; Luebbert 1991). The continental labor movement was primarily a political one. The politicization of the workers' movement was prompted by a general deterioration of economic conditions in the 1880s, and by state repression in most continental countries after the Paris Commune. The popular ideology of the political labor movement was Marxism, which predicted a socialist future on the basis of a well-organized industrial society. The followers of Karl Marx were challenged by anarchists, stressing the need for spontaneous action for a socialist future without any central authority. Related to the rise of the socialist movement was a growing feminist movement stressing women's rights and voting rights in particular.

In 1890, right after the repeal of the anti-socialists law, the German social democratic party founded the General Committee of German Trade Unions (*Generalkommission*). Its aim was to coordinate trade union activities and establish new unions, preferably centralized and national organizations. The unions under the General Committee's wing displayed a large number of activities, including benefits in case of strikes and lockouts, benefits for disabled or unemployed workers, travel reimbursement for workers who had to leave their place of work due to a black list or other employer sanctions, labor exchanges, cultural and educational facilities and cooperatives. The main party demand was general suffrage, and for that reason the unions slowly shifted from craft unionism, confined to skilled workers, to industrial unionism, organizing all workers within a sector, irrespective of their level of training and skills. The goal of general voting rights for all workers made the party gradually trade in its revolutionary aims for a "parliamentary" road towards socialism by means of a socialist victory in elections. The well organized unions contributed to this creeping reformism.

The foundation of the General Committee of German Trade Unions was the union landmark of the late nineteenth century. German influence contributed to similar links between social democratic parties and trade unions in other Germanic countries. The Belgian party also founded a General Commission and in Scandinavia the party and the unions formed a kind of equal partnership from the outset. The main ideas behind this close link were similar to those in Germany: the need for a political struggle to enforce voting rights, and the expectation that this parliamentary road would lead to a socialist majority and ultimately to socialism. This constituted a majority strategy. The majority was not yet there, but it would be reached after the implementation of general voting rights. The expectation of a future majority was fueled by the fast growth of the industrial labor force and by the relative state tolerance of the socialist workers' movement in these countries at the turn of the century. In this Germanic model of trade unionism, the unions formed part of a political movement, but a distinction was made between the political arm of the movement, the party, which pursued political aims, and the industrial or economic arm, the trade unions, which pursued the industrial struggle.

The integration of the unions within a wider movement aiming at a majority in parliament left ample room for a diversity of strategies in dealing with employers. The unions' organizational strength, both towards their members and in contacts with employers, allowed them to engage in collective bargaining, after the example of the craft unions, like that of the printers. This kind of bargaining set fixed terms for the wage rates which were negotiated and implied a no-strike promise for that term, limiting strikes and lockouts to the new bargaining round at the expiration of the existing contract. Since a party appeal for political action might interfere with that "social peace" or "labor peace" obligation, a fierce discussion developed in Germany on the union role in political mass strikes. After a few years the unions gained autonomy from the party. The close link was maintained, but the two would be separate equals, with the party setting the long-term goals and the unions taking care of the "bread and butter" questions and by doing so attracting workers to the movement.

The rise of rival trade unions like Catholic and Protestant ones reinforced the social democrats' strategy. Such movements mainly arose in countries in which Protestants and/or Catholics formed a sizable minority (and in Catholic Belgium). Like the social democratic unions, the Catholic and Protestant unions left the political activities to the Christian Democratic parties and focused on labor conditions.

Mostly in response to the emergence of trade unions, employers set up associations to fight the unions or pressure against labor legislation. The first major clash with the trade unions, in the form of a large strike or lockout, often resulted in a stalemate. The two parties would then seek a solution through collective bargaining. In accordance with their increasing organizational strength the unions, and the employers' associations as well, preferred formal and written agreements. The first agreements were concluded on a local scale in sectors dominated by skilled workers, like printing and the construction industry, soon followed by regional or nationwide agreements in these sectors. In the textile industry, with its large number of unskilled and female labor, and in large enterprises, in particular in the steel industry, employers continued their refusal to recognize the unions.

In Latin Europe a different type of union movement emerged. In France, the Iberian Peninsula and Italy, periods of liberal rule alternated with conservative restoration policies mainly espoused by agrarian interests. Industry was more dispersed over the country, as in France, or concentrated in industrial regions far from the political center, as in Spain (Asturias, Basque country, Catalonia) and Italy (Lombardia, Piemonte). This predominance of separated local or regional labor markets, the regional dispersion of the labor movement and the domination of national politics by vested agrarian interests made it hard for the unions to start a national movement. The industrial dispersion was a more general phenomenon, however, which also applied to Scandinavia.

A second condition, a political one, was even more important in shaping the nature of the labor movement in Latin Europe. Unlike the Germanic countries, the labor movement could hardly count on a majority in parliament. That made the parliamentary road to socialism less promising. The outcome was a small socialist party and a trade union movement which tried to bring about socialism on its own, bypassing the national parliament. This combination of economic and political action made strikes a double-edged weapon, used not only in the struggle against employers but also in the struggle for socialism. Ultimately, a general strike was to be the start of the revolution. The distinction between the economic and the political arenas, which was characteristic of the Germanic labor movement, was rejected. Unions should not, in the Latin European view, impose labor peace upon their members, because doing so would deprive the workers of their only weapon, the strike. They should stimulate spontaneous *action directe*, as the spark would light the general strike that would be at the beginning of the revolution.

The anarchist strategy of *action directe* was based on a long tradition of spontaneous protests of rural workers and of pre-industrial protest in general. While the northern European social democrats regarded their centralized organizations as an innovation, Latin Europe--in part because of the problems that arose in setting up organizations--embraced older and anarchist forms of unorganized protest. Since the unions would play a crucial role in bringing about the revolution and the definite establishment of socialism, this movement was sometimes called anarcho-syndicalist--*syndicat* is French for trade union (Shorter and Tilly 1974).

In contrast to the Germanic majority strategy, this was a minority strategy, pursued by the unions as political actors, but not in the national parliament. The French CGT, founded in 1895 by trade unions and the nationwide body of local labor exchanges, laid down this strategy in its Charter of Amiens. Discussion of parliamentary politics was banned from its meetings as a source of discord and friction. The general strike (*la grève générale*) was not regarded as a political strategy, but as a revolutionary strategy bypassing parliamentary politics. However, the unions were a place of fierce political discussion between anarchists, anarcho-syndicalists, revolutionary Marxists advocating a strong organization and reformist social democrats. In northern Europe the discussion on the political or long-term strategy was left to the party, while in Latin Europe the economic and political struggles were intimately linked, if not identical. The railway workers probably formed the symbol of this combination. They played a crucial role in any large strike, not just those in Latin Europe, since they could spread the news, and any action in the railways was a threat to the national economy and challenged the national government (Geary 1981).

In Latin Europe, employers' associations emerged on a local basis. The dispersion of industry and, even more, the absence of well-organized unions reduced the need to initiate employers' associations. Moreover, the predominance of small enterprises and middle-class *patrons* prevented strong organizations in France. Because of the absence of strong organizations, employers and unions displayed a greater diversity in dealing with each other than in Germanic Europe. Some engaged in formal bargaining, in particular in the printing industry. Most employers turned down any suggestion for bargaining, arguing that they could not deal with a revolutionary movement.

Thus, at the turn of the century, most continental unions were part of a political movement. In Germanic Europe, they formed a combination with the social democratic parties (and a number of smaller unions with the Christian Democratic parties). The common social democratic goal was general suffrage, but the unions had their own sphere of competence. In Latin Europe the unions actually were a political movement in themselves, fighting capitalism by means of spontaneous actions and ultimately a general strike.

The expansion of socialism was a driving force behind the first wave of social and labor legislation. The measures showed the increased government interest in the working class. The latter was no longer merely a "dangerous class," but a class whose living conditions should be improved. The wave was set in motion by Otto von Bismarck, the conservative German prime minister, in the 1880s. In conjunction with the anti-socialist law, social legislation was a positive way to fight socialism. Laws restricting working time for women and children had previously been passed in a number of countries, but Bismarck's social legislation was revolutionary in that it covered adult men, who supposedly were able to take care of themselves. Bismarck's example was not the only force that prompted the new legislation: there existed also a growing social awareness of the poor living and working conditions of the working class because of the socialist publications. The start of collective bargaining and socialist pressure also contributed to the wave of social policy. It began with social security in the form of obligatory disability benefits, followed by other forms of social security, rules on labor contracts and sometimes even rules on collective bargaining. Social legislation in a broader sense provided standards for health, education and housing, and represented a reaction against the large slums in the industrial cities. Even Latin European unions supported some of the initiatives, but in general socialists (both social democrats and more radical socialists) were very critical of the new laws, denouncing them as halfway attempts. The international socialist priority in social legislation, and in collective bargaining, was the eight-hour workday. This would provide the working class with eight hours for sleep and eight hours for the family and recreation. It was the main demand forwarded by the "Second International," established by socialists in 1899.

In contrast to the continent, the British unions stuck to their priority of craft bargaining. In the 1880s unskilled workers set up their own "general workers" unions and became active within the TUC. This contributed to a politicization of the union movement. Tensions with the Liberal Party about judicial rulings on union affairs, including the political levy, made the unions end the "Lib-Lab" cooperation and establish the Labour Party. The party's goal was to prevent government or judicial interference in labor relations, allowing the unions to do their job of improving labor conditions. It was not a political movement fighting for a new model of society and uniting all workers for that purpose. This set the Labour Party apart from the social democratic parties on the continent, with which it developed close ties, however. From an example of craft unionism for the rest of Europe, Great Britain had become a deviant case. German social democracy was now the leading movement, admired for its organizational strength even by anarchists who rejected the membership discipline it required.

The variation between the three parts of Europe is overstressed here, of course. Luebbert has even pointed to similarities in the nature of the British and the French labor movement. In his view, the early French labor movement complied with the political hegemony of the liberals, in a way comparable to the British "Lib-Lab" cooperation. In return, it got political revenues such as strike legislation. In both Britain and France this led to the labor movements' lack of national cohesion (Luebbert 1991). On the other hand, the degree of politicization of the labor movement remains a major difference between the two countries-- with a very strong impact on the nature of labor relations.

1917-1920: THE RISE OF COMMUNISM

World War I (1914-1918) confirmed and deepened the lines of division between the majority and the minority strategies. Under pressure from the 1917 Russian Revolution and large strike waves, general suffrage (at least for men) was granted in most of Europe at the end of the war. However, the elections turned out to be a disappointment for the social democrats. They did not win a majority, and the transition to socialism had to be postponed. The social democrats did not leave the parliamentary road, but shifted their course towards one of coalition building with Christian Democrats or farmers' parties. These parties only slowly overcame their reluctance to accept the social democrats as coalition partners.

The new social democratic strategy, typical of a strong parliamentary minority, was also advocated by a number of union leaders in Latin Europe. The anarcho-syndicalists and anarchists rejected this kind of reformism, however, and a number of them came under the spell of communism. This may seem surprising in view of the communist stress on a strong and disciplined organization and total devotion to the communist party's cause. However, the anarchists and syndicalists shared with the communists the total rejection of capitalism and of "bourgeois" dominated parliamentary democracy (the communists were represented in parliament, but preferred a revolution by non-parliamentary means). They also abhorred the German social democrats' compliance with the war efforts, and hailed the Russian Revolution as the beginning of a new era. Moreover, the communists only organized the revolutionary zealots in the party, the "vanguard of the proletariat" in Lenin's words. In the communist ideology, the unions, as "transmission belts" of the party, did not need so strict a discipline as long as workers could be mobilized for action.

While in the Germanic union movement the social democrats dominated, the Latin movement split between reformist socialists on the one hand and revolutionary socialists and communists, who admired the new communist order in Russia, on the other. In France the communists became a sizable minority movement after walking out of the CGT. In Italy the major movement remained socialist, but there were active communist cells, which organized factory occupations during the strike wave in the main Fiat plants and other industrial centers. In Spain the anarchist unions remained the largest movement but were also engaged in a fierce debate about joining the international communist movement.

Employers founded national umbrella organizations towards the end of the war, mainly to facilitate contacts with the government. Frightened by the international strike wave following the Russian Revolution, the national governments displayed renewed activity in social legislation and in promoting collective bargaining (Maier 1975). The foundation of the International Labor Organization (ILO) in 1919 also encouraged social legislation. By 1920 almost every European country had eight-hour workday legislation, and in many countries the national government also stimulated sector bargaining either by law or by mandating employer representatives to come to the bargaining table. In Germanic Europe collective bargaining took hold, although many large employers still kept aloof. They had even supported company unions opposing the socialists and subordinated to management, but the socialists were able to eliminate these "yellow unions" in most firms. In Latin Europe, where yellow unions were even more prevalent in large companies, collective bargaining remained an exception. The existence of communist unions or communist cells within other unions did not favor contacts with employers. The communists could interrupt any bargaining with strike calls.

1930-1950: CRISIS, WAR AND RECONSTRUCTION

In 1930 Europe began the darkest chapter in its history, with the economic depression, the Nazi rise to power, the Holocaust, Stalinist terror in Russia and World War II.

The 1930 economic depression affected most countries; unemployment went up to twenty or even thirty percent. The typical response was for governments to devalue the national currency in order to make exports cheaper, to permit cartel-like agreements among employers in order to allocate the remaining production and to set up some employment projects. After their rise to power in 1933 the Nazis set up larger employment programs and stimulated employment through the growing war industry. Conservatives all over Europe admired this firm employment policy, and even more the strict hierarchical order of Nazism. Italy had its own fascist order beginning in the early 1920s and in the course of the 1930s other countries, mainly in Latin and Central Europe, followed. They suppressed all unions and established state-controlled workers organizations, which monopolized bargaining with the employers' associations.

In response to the rise of fascist dictatorships and German expansionism, the Russians ordered communists in other countries to abandon their isolation and seek new forms of understanding with socialists. In France such a socialist-communist "Popular Front" won the 1936 elections and was welcomed by a large strike wave, which resulted in the Accord Matignon. In Spain the Popular Front called forth an armed fascist reaction, leading to the Spanish Civil War (1936-1939). In that war fascist Italy and Nazi Germany supported the fascist cause, while international communists and radical socialists supported the Popular Front.

A number of Germanic countries, affected by the depression and terrified by the expansion of fascism and growing international tension, sought new ways to secure at least a more lasting national labor peace. The resulting national labor truces--like the Norwegian 1935 Basic Agreement, the Swedish 1938 Saltsjöbaden Agreement and a formal peace treaty (*Friedensvertrag*) concluded in the Swiss metal industry in 1937--represented the beginning of corporatism.

During World War II, unions were suppressed under German occupation. Socialists and communists were under attack. After the war, social democrats provided the leadership in the reconstruction process in the smaller Germanic countries. They introduced state monitoring of the economy, as advocated by the British liberal John Maynard Keynes. Keynesian "demand management" included anti-cyclical steering of the economy by increasing the demand side in times of recession--for instance by transfer payments and social security for the lower income groups, who would consume more of their income than high-income groups. In times of an overheated economy additional taxes would reduce demand. During the period of reconstruction most countries also imposed strict wage and price policies. The notion of a national consensus for the reconstruction effort, Keynesian economic policy and the strict wage and price policy encouraged the start or the revival of corporatism.

Nationalization of large enterprises ranked high on the list of social democratic demands. Especially in Germany it was motivated by the desire to prevent any new war mongering, but in that country the British and American Allied Forces rejected nationalization. In the smaller Germanic countries the unions did not wholeheartedly support nationalization of industrial companies. Instead, they stressed a bargaining relationship with the employers. In France and Italy communists had joined the resistance movement after the German invasion of Russia. Supported by their tightly knit resistance networks they became the leaders in postwar "national fronts," which also included socialists. The national front governments nationalized a number of large enterprises, whose managers were convicted of common cause with the fascists and Nazis. The resulting large public sectors, especially the nationalized Renault automobile works in France, were to play a prominent role in postwar labor relations.

The beginning of the Cold War in 1947-1948, in which the American Marshall Plan was a significant issue, changed the political climate in Europe and reinforced the division between Germanic and the Latin labor relations. It brought forth a reaction against state intervention in the economy and a reappraisal of free enterprise and free bargaining. In that social climate the German Federal Republic was founded in 1948. In most countries strict wage and price control was given up, but Keynesian economic policy was continued. In France and Italy the communists, dominating the largest union confederations (the CGT in France and the CGIL in Italy) left the national government. As a consequence, collective bargaining remained either exceptional or was frequently interrupted by the unions' political actions. The Iberian Peninsula continued to be ruled by the fascist dictatorships installed in the 1930s. State-controlled trade unions engaged in bargaining with relatively autonomous employers' associations.

British labor relations were less affected by both world wars and the Cold War. The system of labor relations, based on craft unions and state abstention, was continued, but the unions became more involved in politics and became supporters of social legislation. A number of core industrial sectors, like mining and the steel industry, were nationalized as the only means to provide sufficient investment funds.

In addition to Keynesianism, one of the novelties in postwar European social legislation was the extension of social security to the entire population. This "universal coverage" was advocated by William Beveridge, like Keynes a British liberal. Social democrats on the continent became the main advocates of Keynesian economic policy and Beveridgian social security.

1960-1974: THE GOLDEN SIXTIES

The expanding car industry, electronics and the chemical industry were the leading sectors in this period. Oil replaced coal as the main source of fuel, and coal mines were being closed. The center of industry shifted from traditional mining areas like the Ruhr area, Wallony in Belgium, Lorraine in France, and northern England to major ports like Rotterdam, Hamburg, Antwerp, Marseilles and Genoa, with petrochemical industries as the symbols of progress. The internationalization of the economy was expressed in expanding U.S. investments in European industry and in the foundation of a number of European agencies to coordinate economic and energy policies, the beginning of the European Union. "Fordism," the combination of mass production and mass consumption, regulated the economy, with productivity increase as the leading principle. It gave rise to a continuous process of economic restructuring and to permanent wage increases, linked to the productivity growth. National governments followed the process with anti-cyclical Keynesian policies. A sharp rise in social security served not only this economic demand management but also the social ideal of more equality. Full employment, high and increasing wages, high social security expenditure, and increasing state spending on health, housing and education made the 1960s the zenith of the "Welfare State." In accordance with Keynesian policies, wage bargaining became more centralized, with the link between wages and productivity as the guiding principle. The unions stressed more equality, especially between high-productivity and low-productivity sectors and regions and between manual and clerical workers. The "golden sixties," symbolized by the enormous spread of private cars, showed some convergence between the Germanic and the Latin model of labor relations. Collective bargaining expanded, and in spite of a tight labor market the strike rate declined due to the link between wages and productivity. The idea took root that strikes were a relic of the past, mainly confined to "outdated" sectors like mining. Industrial restructuring to increase productivity stimulated worker mobility and retraining, as well as an increase in the numbers of clerical workers in industry and services. Immigrant workers filled the vacancies for manual labor.

The May 1968 revolt by Paris students interrupted this period of productivity-based bargaining. It started an international protest movement directed against any form of traditional authority, including trade union leaders. The unions saw themselves confronted with large spontaneous strikes and responded to the strikes by decentralizing collective bargaining and demanding more worker participation within enterprises. Employers tried to stop the movement in the traditional way, by offering higher wages. Initially, France in 1968 (Constat de Grenelle) and Italy in 1969 (*autunno caldo*) constituted the main locations for the wave of spontaneous, and later also union-organized, strikes. In the early 1970s the wave expanded to most Germanic countries, where workers and unions had to wait until the current labor agreements expired. Large strikes in the iron ore mines of northern Sweden, German automobile works, the Dutch port of Rotterdam, and Belgian coal mines were expressions of the new worker militancy.

To some observers, this continental strike wave was the beginning of a new era of worker militancy, if not the start of the revolution. They proved to be wrong, but the immediate gains for workers were great, with large improvements in labor conditions. Worker participation was extended and wages and social security benefits rose quickly, as did state spending on social policies (Crouch and Pizzorno 1978). The public sector, with growing numbers of workers in education and health care, became a major employer. The protest movement affected religious organizations, including Catholic unions. The Catholic unions in the Low Countries and in France stressed their autonomy from the Catholic Church, followed by a process of radicalization. A second feminist movement (the first occurred at the turn of the century) also sprang up during this period. It claimed equal rights for women and advocated more female participation in the labor market. The tight labor market and the expansion of clerical work and the public sector also stimulated female participation.

The fast rise in oil prices during the first oil crisis in 1974 brought an end to this period of rising expectations. Stagflation, a combination of growing unemployment and inflation, could no longer be cured by Keynesian state intervention in the economy.

CENTRAL EUROPE UNDER COMMUNISM

The early labor movement in Central Europe, most of it under Russian and Austro-Hungarian rule until World War I, had faced the same problems as in Latin Europe but was influenced more by the German socialists than by anarchism. They actively tried to set up a well-organized revolutionary movement in order to combine participation in parliamentary politics (where that was being developed) and to lead the revolution. One of the distinctive features of the labor movement in Central Europe was its nationalism, stressing national independence in combination with international socialism. Employers' associations were rare. The only sector in which collective bargaining developed was in the printing industry.

After World War I a number of new nations gained independence, but only Czechoslovakia developed a strong labor movement, more or less similar to the Germanic ones. The other countries were plagued by recurrent dictatorships in the 1920s and 1930s. The rise of Nazism in Germany provided a new pretext for dictators to impose authoritarian rule, sometimes including some Catholic corporatist or state-corporatist ideas.

During World War II the Western Allies left Central Europe to the Russians. After the start of the Cold War Russia imposed its communist model of politics and labor relations. In that political system the communist party possessed a virtual power monopoly. It controlled all social and political institutions, including the national government, as well as the economy, consisting of nationalized enterprises subject to central planning directives. Total party control forced the unions to function as "transmission belts" of the party, which left workers without an organization of their own to protect them against the state, or better, against the party. The argument was that Russia had become a workers' state after the 1917 revolution. It had done away with capitalism and had brought the communist party into power, the "vanguard of the proletariat." In order to prevent a return to pre-revolutionary times, the proletariat had to install the "dictatorship of the proletariat" (another Leninist term) for a number of years. Since the dictatorship was actually exercised by the party, which institution, by definition, met the workers' interests, workers did not need any other organization. Furthermore, the existence of autonomous organizations, not under communist control, undermined the proletariat's power and endangered the accomplishments of the revolution. Although the unions engaged in collective bargaining with state enterprises and voiced some objections against harsh and arbitrary labor rules, their main concern was "worker exhortation." This encouraged workers to work harder in order to turn Russia into a fully industrialized country and to create the material foundations of communism. The communist obsession with discipline, order and hierarchy permeated all aspects of social life, especially under Josef Stalin.

The same industrialization policy was pursued in central Europe. Cracks became visible now and then, with national revolts against the Russian domination and against intolerable labor conditions. Major revolts took place in Poland and Hungary in 1956, the latter crushed by the Russian army. To deal with this protest and to soften the rigidities of central planning, economic planning was decentralized to some extent in the 1960s. Workers' councils were established in factories, sometimes in response to the spread of spontaneous workers' councils that had emerged at the times of revolt. A second military invasion, in Czechoslovakia in 1968, ended efforts of democratization in that country.

In the 1970s Hungary became the first country to slowly move away from the Leninist and Stalinist type of trade unions and to give them a say in labor conditions, thus allowing more room for collective bargaining. In 1980 a large autonomous trade union movement, Solidarność, sprang up in Poland, but the overall democratization of political and social life did not begin until the end of the 1980s. By that time the Russian leader Mikhail Gorbachev had started a campaign of more openness (*glasnost*) and social reconstruction (*perestroika*), which had the effect, however, of undermining the power monopoly of the communist party. The ossified structure of Russian society under communism, with its very bad economic performance, blatant corruption, and lack of legitimacy, did not stand this change and collapsed. The result was the demise of international communism, the end of Soviet Russian domination of Central Europe and the reunification of Germany.

Central Europe has embarked upon a difficult course towards democratization and privatization of the economy. It has developed close ties with Western Europe and is looking at Western European examples of free unionism and labor relations, as examples for "national" roads of development.

4

Labor Relations and Politics in the 1990s

The 1974 oil crisis was followed by a second one in 1979-1980. They gave rise to inflation and to unemployment, which caused a shift in power towards the employers. Changes in the composition of the labor force have also affected trade unions and union-party relations. In the 1980s and 1990s a number of economic and political changes have been weakening both trade unions and social democratic parties. Once a solid bloc, the social democratic movement has become a more uneasy combination of two partners who have stuck together because of their common struggle in the past rather than their plans for the future. In Latin Europe and Central Europe even more powerful forces have been at work, such as the demise of international communism, which forced communist-dominated unions to redefine their place in society in competition with other union and political movements.

TECHNOLOGY AND THE LABOR MARKET

In the 1960s most continental unions upheld the almost permanent process of rationalization as a sign of progress, leading to higher productivity and wage increase. Unemployment was reduced to shorter periods of friction between plant closure and placement in more productive plants. In the early 1970s rationalization became a target of worker militancy, in which protests were raised against the impact of technological change on employment and social life in general. The two oil crises and Japan's rise as a leading industrial power have reinforced the process of economic structuring. Japanese cars, TV sets and audio racks flood the European market. European industry is trying to reduce labor costs and to keep in pace with the Japanese labor productivity. This is a difficult task since in Japan productivity is higher and wages lower, and the Japanese market is relatively closed for European products (HBS 1992; Tokunaga, Altmann, and Demes 1992). Due to the Japanese challenge and the growth of unemployment, the restructuring, rationalization, and even the "robotization" of industry meet with little worker protest. Non-compliance with the technological standards set by Japan would mean even more unemployment (Michie and Smith 1994).

The rationalization of industry has caused a decrease in manual work. The labor force in the steel industry, textiles, shipbuilding and in other large-scale industries has declined. European industry is not only being rationalized, it is also subject to increasing international capital mobility (Notermans 1993; Moses 1993). Parts of industrial production move to low-wage countries, in particular to East Asia. For older workers various types of early retirement schemes have been set up, younger workers stay longer in school and more people are trained for clerical work in industry. In the mid-1990s less than forty percent, and in many countries even less than thirty percent, of the labor force is still employed in industry.

De-industrialization and the decline of the industrial labor force are compensated only to some extent by a rise in the number of commercial service workers. The continuous income increases in the 1960s and 1970s gave rise to an expansion of banking facilities, insurance schemes and, most of all, to a recreation "industry." The two oil crises did not halt its growth, since early retirement schemes and shorter working time were popular union strategies to fight growing unemployment and better allocate work. Short holiday weekends stimulated recreational services in northern Europe and longer holidays the beach resorts in Latin Europe and air transport throughout Europe. The growing commercial service sector mainly employs clerical workers and workers who regard themselves as middle class rather than working class. This growth of clerical jobs in commercial services has contributed even more than the shift within industry to the change from manual to clerical work.

The service sector contains yet another component, in the form of public, or at least non-commercial services (sometimes called the fourth sector, in addition to agriculture, industry and commercial services). In particular education, health care and social security have been growth sectors. Education started to grow in the late 1950s and 1960s, when most workers no longer thought of their children as followers in their footsteps. School age was extended to fourteen or sixteen, and universities expanded in order to house the "baby boom" generation born right after the war, including a growing proportion of students from working-class origins. Health care and social security bureaucracies followed as parts of the European welfare state. As sources of employment they are still growing and seem to have an even brighter future than education, due to the growing life expectancy and the increasing proportion of "senior citizens" in the population. These non-commercial services are either state provided or at least partly state financed. Like the commercial services, they mainly employ clerical workers or workers identifying with the middle class, like nurses. The combination of commercial and non-commercial services now makes up a majority of the labor force in almost every European country and even a two-thirds majority in Great Britain, France, and most corporatist nations. In contrast to these countries, the German economy continues to be based upon industry.

Three trends have been mentioned: The shift from manual to clerical work in industry, the rise of commercial services, and the growth of non-commercial services, with both the commercial and non-commercial service sectors predominantly employing clerical workers. In addition, two other changes have affected the labor force--gender composition and national origin.

Throughout Europe the number of women on the labor market has steadily increased. In addition to the tight labor market of the 1960s, the expansion of office work contributed to this growth. It provided a kind of employment which was deemed to be acceptable for middle-class girls and women, and a means of upward social mobility for working class girls. The second feminist movement of the early 1970s further opened up opportunities for women. In Scandinavia, where over seventy percent of all women have paid jobs, stimulating the female participation rate has been an integral part of labor market policies. In other countries it was discouraged as part of a Catholic family policy, but the increase in opportunities for clerical work and the changing attitudes towards paid work by women caused a shift in the 1970s and 1980s (Castles 1994). Only in a few countries, mainly in Latin Europe, the majority of women does not have paid jobs. In the other countries many of them are employed in part-time functions, stimulated by the general trend towards flexi-time (Rubery and Fagan 1994).

The last change in the labor force composition has been the growth in the number of foreign workers. This is not a new phenomenon. Many Irish immigrant workers were employed in British railroad construction in the nineteenth century, while Central and Latin Europeans worked in Belgian, French and German coal mines and steelworks in the early twentieth century. In the early 1960s most immigrants came from Latin Europe. Portuguese and Spanish workers went to France and Germany; within Italy there was a migration flow from the rural south to the industrialized north. The recruitment policies of France and northern Europe soon extended to countries outside Europe, in particular North Africa (Morocco and Algeria) and Turkey. Migrants from North Africa especially went to France and Turkish migrants to Germany. They were mainly recruited for unskilled manual work and filled the vacancies left by native workers who made the shift towards skilled and clerical work. The concentration of the immigrant workers, the *Gastarbeiter* as they are called in Germany, in unskilled industrial work has made them early victims of unemployment since the 1970s. They have also become easy scapegoats for rising unemployment, the more so since they have brought their families with them, display a different cultural background in (the Islamic) religion, education and gender relations, and poorly integrate into society (Baldwin-Edwards and Schain 1994). The arguments used against their continued stay are either that they occupy jobs which should be filled by native workers or that they are "idle" and merely "enjoying" unemployment pay. Despite checks upon immigration, the share of people from foreign origins in the total European population is still rising, in part due to a larger family size.

The shift from a manual to a clerical labor force and the increase in female and immigrant labor has affected the trade unions in various ways. First, the unions are experiencing slow membership growth or even a decline in the unionization rate. Previously, manual workers in industry, eager to unionize and also relatively easy to mobilize for action, made up the backbone of the trade unions. Clerical workers have a considerably lower unionization rate. Traditionally, they are more oriented towards a professional career and a relationship with the firm than with union solidarity. Many female workers carry a double burden (paid job and houshold activities), and partly for that reason are also less unionized than men, in particular when they work in part-time jobs. Immigrant workers have been hard to organize since they are not familiar with trade unionism and fear employer sanctions. A number of Moroccan immigrants have even faced sanctions in their home country for union activities in Europe. The union priorities, of course, also contribute to the lower unionization rate among clerical, female and immigrant workers. Only in Sweden is the unionization rate of clerical workers and women at the same level or even higher than that of manual workers, due to a very active recruitment policy among female office employees. In the rest of Europe, only one category of clerical workers has been eager to organize, the higher educated workers in the public services. In public services union activities do not interfere with a career and may even be an asset for promotion.

As a consequence of the decline or the stabilization of their membership numbers, and in order to attract new members, the trade unions are increasingly stressing their capacity as service institutions, providing legal assistance and other forms of support. This means that they have come to stress individual incentives to join rather than social solidarity as a "natural" base of trade union membership. Only a few nations have avoided this union decline. In Finland the membership rate has even shown a sharp rise, due to the unification of the union movement in 1969 and a gradual transition to a system of centralized collective bargaining and corporatism similar to that in Scandinavia during the 1970s and 1980s.

The second effect of the labor market changes on trade unions has been that industrial workers' unions have lost their predominant position within the trade union confederations to clerical workers' unions or public sector unions. In many countries the largest union member in the national confederation is now either a clerical workers' union, as in Denmark, or a public sector union, as in Holland. The most conspicuous exception is Germany. Due to the continued large size of the German industrial labor force, IG Metall (*Industriegewerkschaft Metall*)--which covers the steel industry, machine construction and car manufacture--is still by far the largest DGB member union. With its three million members, one-third of the total DGB membership, including clerical workers, it is also the largest single European union.

A third effect consists of the rise or the expansion of new clerical workers' confederations and public sector confederations, which affect the position of the existing peak organizations. In some countries separate union organizations for middle and higher echelon workers, university trained employees and "cadre," though the latter term denotes a different category in each country, are also on the rise. Such independent confederations of clerical workers and higher echelon employees exist even in Scandinavia. They increasingly challenge the power monopoly of the general union confederations in those countries.

The strong focus on the unionization rate in labor relations literature has often led to the conclusion that a decline in numbers implies a loss of trade union power. A direct relationship between size and power is doubtful. But declining numbers affect the unions' capacity to be active in the workplace, and such activities are an important means to recruit new members. Membership strength might also affect the unions' ability to mobilize workers for actions. These effects are felt throughout Europe (Visser 1992).

The labor force changes have also had a large impact on the social democratic parties in Germanic countries. Previously, union membership and a social democratic vote was a natural combination, but this is no longer true. Already in the 1950s social democratic parties started to broaden their electoral base in order to attract middle-class voters. For that reason the German party gave up its marxist ideology in its 1959 "Bad Godesberg Program." These efforts to become broad "catch-all" parties did not affect social democracy's traditional base--the manual workers in industry. The new clerical labor force, however, lacks the propensity to vote strictly social democrat. They are more divided, voting either for social democratic, Christian Democratic, liberal, conservative parties, or are "floating voters." The immigrant workers have not compensated for that loss. Many of them are still without voting rights, and even when they do have the right to vote, they often abstain.

Even worse, many of the traditional social democratic voters no longer regard such a vote as obvious. Social solidarity has lost its appeal and has been replaced by other political concerns, a more calculating attitude, or a different view of the social and economic policies needed. Social democrats have gradually lost votes, giving way to conservative and center-right governments in the early 1980s. The Labour Party has shared that fate and has been unable to turn the tide of manual workers voting for the Conservative Party. The same applies to the declining propensity of Latin European workers to vote communist and to support communist-inspired actions. This is also due to the demise of international communism, to be discussed below. The decline of social democracy in Germanic Europe is a completely indigenous phenomenon. It is reflected in book titles like *The Future of Social Democracy*, *The Crisis of Socialism*, and *The End of Socialism* (Paterson and Thomas 1986).

Employers' associations have been particularly affected by the rise of the public sector. Their bargaining monopoly has been lost. In the 1970s   the national governments became the largest employer, deciding labor conditions for a sizable proportion of the labor force. In Belgium, employers in the commercial services and in industry have refused employers in the non-commercial services access to tripartite councils. They believe the latter are too dependent upon government funding and, as a consequence, would reinforce the governments' influence in such councils.

The changes have had a large impact on the political scene in Europe. In Great Britain, conservative governments have been in power since 1979, and Prime Minister Margaret Thatcher especially took a fierce anti-union stance in the 1980s. In Scandinavia, conservative and liberal cabinets took over one or more times in the early 1980s. In Sweden such a government was formed in 1976, after decades of social democratic governments. Social democrats, however, had reclaimed power in a number of countries at the end of the 1980s and the early 1990s, albeit in weaker positions than in the 1960s and 1970s. Germany is the only Germanic country in which social democrats been out of power since the early 1980s, as in Britain.

British labor relations have been even more deeply affected by these changes than by the two world wars. The Conservative governments of the 1980s broke the traditional insulation of labor relations from politics in favor of legal curbs on trade union activities, and a series of labor laws in the course of the 1980s explicitly aimed at restricting trade union practices. Moreover, even the Labour opposition has slowly come to accept these measures and has refrained from or withdrawn traditional pledges to undo such conservative laws, once it attains power again. Latin European labor relations have also been subject to great change, with communist trade unions losing hold. The Germanic model has been less affected, because of the distinction between political and industrial strategies. However, the position of the national government in the Germanic model has been under stress, due to changing economic conditions.

THE ECONOMY AND THE GOVERNMENT

The combination of unemployment and inflation (stagflation) which struck a number of countries after the 1974 oil crisis seemed to ask for a new kind of crisis management. National governments intensified their contacts with trade unions and employers in order to discuss strategies to cope with the crisis. Neo-corporatism flourished. Employers and unions, however, were divided over the policies to be pursued. While unions proposed stronger Keynesian intervention to reduce unemployment, employers advocated the fight against inflation. They pointed to rising wage demands, influenced by the price rises but far ahead of productivity gains. Some governments then interfered in wage bargaining. After the 1979-80 oil crisis unemployment became the overriding problem. In some countries it rose to over ten percent; in others the increase was slower. However, only a few nations were able to keep unemployment at the pre-1980 level, notably Sweden and Austria--which stimulated the discussion on corporatism as an anti-unemployment strategy. The main strategy in both countries was to expand the public sector.

Neither this expansion nor Keynesianism in general proved a solution; rather, they mainly increased the budget deficits. New economic ideas gained popularity, stating that the welfare state had expanded beyond limits. The free market had been curbed too much, high unemployment pay had reduced the incentive to work and rising minimum wages had affected the mobility of the labor market. The heavy tax burden had reduced private initiative and high state expenditure with falling tax receipts had caused a growing budget deficit. The leading "hawk" for this new line of thinking was British Conservative Prime Minister Margaret Thatcher, who blamed the unions as the main cause of economic decline and productivity loss. In other countries the unions also came under attack because of the rigidities they imposed on the labor market (Koelble 1988).

Even more than the unions, the national governments were regarded as a source of evil. They had grown out of proportion and the far-too-large public sector killed any initiative--not only within the services belonging to it but also in the private sector. Deregulation and privatization became the catchwords of the 1980s and 1990s, and they continue to be high government priorities in most of Europe (Mueller and Wright 1994). The conservative and center-right governments in power in the 1980s, partly voted in power by trade union members, at first intensified their intervention in the economy to lay the base for deregulation and to impose wage restraint. The new policies have met with union opposition, but many governments no longer bother much about tripartism and consensus building. The budget deficits, unemployment and the lack of union-employer agreement all call for immediate action. Even when employers and unions are able to forward common proposals, the national governments sometimes neglect them in favor of measures which reduce the deficit (Compston 1994; Kurzer 1991), "no-nonsense" policy, as it is called in Holland. However, increased government initiative also includes efforts to bring employers and trade unions together for talks about wage moderation and other topics. This happened in Germany in January 1996, when the national confederations--in an exceptional example of national bargaining--laid down a number of general principles for sector wage bargaining, with the aim of halting unemployment growth. The principles included reduction of wage costs, lower social security contributions and a greater flexibility in working time. This national "pact" almost amounted to a tripartite agreement because of the government's involvement and the continuation of the talks afterwards about the elaboration of the measures.

As a result of this increase in government activities and the shift in the smaller nations from corporatism to more government initiative, the position of the national government has become a more disputed one, straining the relationship with the trade unions. The unions have called demonstrations and also sporadic strikes against state policies, even when social democratic parties participate in government. Labor relations in the Germanic model have become politicized, but that process has been limited by two other developments. First, both the conservative governments of the early 1980s and the governments of the 1990s in which social democrats participate no longer offer anything in return for wage restraint. They are able to reach the goal of wage restraint by having the organizations themselves do the job, and they can point to the need for budget cuts. As a consequence, the unions are no longer able to use the political strategies as they did in the early 1970s. Second, and more important, neither the unions nor social democratic parties form a closed front. Trade unions in the private sector slowly have come to appreciate a number of deregulation measures, that could contribute to productivity growth. In contrast, the large public sector unions generally resist deregulation and privatization of state enterprises as an attack upon their position.

The disagreement between private and public sector unions has been aggravated by government efforts to impose wage restraint in the public sector to serve as an example for the rest of the economy. This has resulted in protest action in the areas of health care, education and public transport, but protest has been confined to public sector unions. Private sector and public sector unions still join hand in protest against statutory wage policies and against cuts in social security and in public services. They have drifted apart in the matters of privatization and wage restraint in the public sector, which are strongly opposed by the public sector unions; private sector unions favor the measures or take a neutral stance. In the eyes of the other unions public sector workers merely defend their privileged position of greater job security. The more radical position of the public sector unions has not only been attributed to the decline in member privileges, and in job security in particular, but also to the relatively high level of education of members, more ideologically motivated and more vociferous about what they consider to be an attack on the whole labor movement.

The same line of division runs through social democratic parties, which at first stuck to Keynesianism. The public sector workers even contributed to a radicalization of social democracy, but after disastrous election results in the late 1970s and early 1980s the social democratic parties revised their position in order to win back middle-class votes and, in particular, clerical workers. They no longer oppose privatization and deregulation, and they have even shifted from support for "state care" to "individual responsibility." In countries where social democrats returned to power, or were readmitted to government as coalition partners in the late 1980s, they supported cuts in state budget and privatization programs. They are divided, however, between small groups of well-educated leftists, who are based in the public sector and oppose the "new realism," and a majority drifting towards a position of less state power. The parties have not yet been able to find a new paradigm. They speak about less state control but do not yet know what else to advocate. This internal division reduces the electoral support of the parties, especially since the open character of social democratic parties allows for much publicity around congresses and party meetings (Scharpf 1990; Swenson 1992).

Since the late 1980s national governments have again been engaged in efforts to reduce their involvement in labor relations in a number of ways: less social legislation, less compensatory measures in return for wage restraint, privatization of state services and decentralization of private sector bargaining. All of this is aimed at creating a more flexible labor market and a return to the previously undisputed position of the national government in labor relations: one of sanctioning bargaining rather than pursuing a leading course in wage policies and public sector employment (Crouch 1994).

While the changes in the labor market have affected the unions' size and bargaining power, the change in the political climate has undermined the position of the unions in central level talks and tripartism. Union advice is no longer sought, and their compliance is effectuated anyway by the economic conditions and the continued high unemployment levels.

In Latin Europe the national economies have been subjected to the same forces--like attempts at government intervention in wage bargaining, cuts in public expenditure and privatization--with similar results. In France a short period of Keynesian policies and social legislation in the early 1980s soon gave way to a shift in policies and to new conservative governments, even under the socialist president Francois Mitterand. The effect of these conservative measures has been an even stronger split between public sector union militancy and acquiescence in the rest of the economy. While private sector union power and militancy are in decline, even more so in Latin Europe than in Germanic Europe, the public sector has become the bearer of protest against cuts in state spending and privatization, as exemplified by the large strikes in France at the end of 1995. The actions started among the railroad workers to fight a change in their retirement provisions and soon expanded to the rest of the public sector, fighting general cuts in social security. Despite the paralyzation of French public life for over three weeks, there was some general sympathy with the action but workers in the private sector refused to join the strikers.

The decline in mobilizing power in the private sector affects the Latin unions more than it does the Germanic ones, where such mobilization is less of a union concern. The difference between private and public sector unions is not just one of moderation versus more radical claims, but one of force, with the private sector unions sunk into disarray and the public sector unions emerging as the last stronghold of worker militancy. This difference also stems from developments which have had a uniquely large impact on Latin Europe, the end of fascism and the decline of communism.

THE END OF DICTATORSHIP AND THE DEMISE OF COMMUNISM IN LATIN EUROPE

Latin Europe and Central Europe have been subject to more profound political change than has Germanic Europe. In the Iberian Peninsula the long period of fascism came to an end in the mid-1970s. Communists already dominated the illegal workers' committees and organizations that had been set up before. Socialists reestablished their own pre-fascist trade union movement. The Spanish socialist union confederation was strongly supported by the governing socialist party, and partly financed by the German social democrats. A period of uneasy cooperation and more overt conflict between the unions followed. While the socialists stressed collective bargaining, in imitation of Germanic Europe, the communist-dominated movements were more politically oriented and acted as a kind of political opposition movement. They demanded more active employment policies (unemployment in Spain had reached twenty percent) and resisted any reduction of formal job security rights, one of the few workers' rights under fascism. In Portugal a short-lived 1974 socialist revolution brought an end to the long period of fascist dictatorship and resulted in a large expansion of the public sector through the nationalization of industries. Since then, the communists have tried to stop attempts to dismantle this public sector. A short period of dictatorship in Greece also ended in the mid-1970s, but in that country the major union confederation remained dominated by the socialist party.

Because of their orientation towards national problems of economic transition, the communist-dominated unions on the Iberian Peninsula are less affected than the Italian and the French trade union movements by the demise of international communism. In the latter two countries the total political expression of workers' demands is at stake, including not only trade unionism but also a more long-standing political orientation of the working class towards the communist parties. In France the socialist party has been able to take over, but it has remained strongly divided by a number of ideological trends, each of them often concentrated around one party leader. The French trade union movement has dwindled to a density of less than ten percent, and in French works council elections--the most used yardstick to measure relative support for the unions--non-unionized candidates have become the largest category. In Italy the trade unions fare better, but the political system is in complete disarray, because of widespread corruption, ties between prominent Christian Democratic and socialist politicians and the Mafia and the failure of newly arisen political parties to change the system.

The impact of these political and social changes is much greater than in Germanic Europe. First, the political changes in Germanic Europe consist of internal shifts within the group of parties that make up the government most of the time. Social democrats are losing, while conservatives and liberals gain seats. In Latin Europe the decline of communism affects the political system as such. It implies a shift from a non-parliamentary or even anti-parliamentary orientation represented by the communist party towards parties that are integrated in the political system. The Spanish socialists have even become the main pillar of the parliamentary system, while in France labor politics have become parliamentary politics with the rise of the socialist party. The role of the communist movement as a large, partly non-parliamentary opposition movement is dead, which opens a road for a succession of labor-oriented and non-labor-oriented governments, as in Germanic Europe and Britain. At the same time a new anti-parliamentarism is on the rise, in the form of the French *Front National* and Italian neo-fascism and similar movements in Germanic Europe.

Second, labor legislation in Latin Europe has often been enforced by strike movements. This tradition is also under challenge, since either the mobilization force of the unions has been seriously affected or socialists are in power, but without much room for sweeping reform. This reduces the Latin unions' involvement in politics. They no longer form a sizable protest force outside the system, nor do they have strong links with parties in government, except in Spain. National politics and tripartism is becoming less promising for labor in Germanic Europe, but Latin labor's role in politics and in pressure for legislation has been reduced even more, leaving the enterprise level as a new field of activity.

In Spain and Portugal there have been attempts to develop tripartism and to establish tripartite councils. Spain has also had a number of peak-level agreements in the early 1980s, some of them without the participation or signature of the communist-dominated union movement. In neither country has tripartism become an important feature of labor relations, however. Neither partiy has been willing to tie its own hands, and the communist-dominated unions in particular are not ready to de-politicize issues at hand, preferring to maintain union-government conflict as a base of political mobilization. This also applies to the socialist Greek unions.

NEW LABOR RELATIONS IN CENTRAL EUROPE

In Central Europe the changes have been far more sweeping than in Western Europe. Political life has been democratized and there is a gradual transition towards private enterprises and free market economies. One of the measures promoting this development is the privatization of state enterprises. Meanwhile, labor relations are slowly emerging as a field of activity which is distinct from politics and in which several types of organizations play a role.

In some countries the communist trade unions have transformed themselves into "post-communist" union organizations, looking for new ideals in Germanic social democracy and Latin socialism and especially active in resisting privatization. An exception to this top-down transformation of communist into post-communist unions is Czechia. In that country (before the division of Czechoslovakia into Czechia and Slovakia) spontaneous strike committees were formed at the end of the communist period. They took over the weakened communist unions, which clung to their traditional role, and turned them into a kind of social democratic union movement. In other countries new movements also sprang up in the late 1980s, after the example of Poland's Solidarność. In Bulgaria and Hungary a number of these new union confederations exist, including unions specifically appealing to clerical workers and to workers' council members. In all these countries the transformed communist movement has remained by far the largest one, however, due in part to its extensive social provisions and assets. The division of these assets became a hot issue in the early 1990s, as the new organizations claimed their fair share.

Not surprising, employers' associations were slow to arise. Most large industries continue to be state owned or state controlled, although various forms of privatization are on the way. Free enterprise is mainly dominated by foreign multinationals and by small indigenous entrepreneurs, which is not a very strong base for employers' associations. Managers of state-controlled industries act as leaders in the employers' associations, but they are neither entrepreneurs nor autonomous from the state. In some countries regional "Chambers of Commerce," organized by industrial branch, which were responsible for inter-sector trade and for exports under communism, are playing a role as "new" employers' associations.

A number of Central European countries are currently experimenting with tripartite institutions. In Hungary and Czechia tripartite councils have been established. Bulgaria has probably tried hardest and has already seen a succession of three tripartite bodies, as well as the introduction of regional and branch councils. The councils try to perform three distinct functions. They act as consultants to the national government, as national bargaining institutions that negotiate national agreements and as arbitrators or mediators in labor disputes (Héthy 1994). The first two functions also apply to Germanic corporatism, while the third function is less common for tripartite bodies. The councils can point to a number of successes in all functions, including consultation on the new labor laws that provide frameworks for new systems of labor relations. Several countries passed this kind of legislation in the early 1990s. The councils also face serious problems, however, which make them fall short of real tripartism as discussed in Chapter 1.

First, employers' associations are still in their infant stage and their development is to some extent dependent upon the pace of the privatization process carried out by the national governments. The weakness of the employers' organizations often leads national governments to discuss major economic and social problems with the trade unions only or to take measures without any prior consultation.

Second, the trade unions have not stabilized their position. The union density has declined from over ninety percent under communism to less than fifty percent. This may be a "normal" development, but it is unclear at what level union density will stabilize. Moreover, except in Czechia, the union movement is highly divided between the strong "old" confederation and one or more "new" movements. Even where the issue of union assets has been solved, the unions oppose each other on a large number of issues, including the pace of privatization and the state policies during the transformation period. They also differ in their ties with political parties. Some of the unions maintain good contacts with political parties represented in government or with parties that have a good chance to be represented. Even on that point any definite conclusions are hardly possible, due to the great fluctuations in the strength of the political parties. There also exists a great variation in the social base of the movements. Some of the new unions are hardly more than loose coalitions of groups of militant workers within a small number of enterprises, and they may easily fall apart (Moerel 1994).

Third, the national governments are leading a process towards economic transformation, an even more profound change than the postwar economic reconstruction in Western Europe. Mounting problems have to be handled, including unemployment and inflation. Workers were used to a high degree of job security under communism, which implied forms of "hidden unemployment." Unemployment has now risen to over ten percent, and industrial adaptation to the standards of international competition has given rise to strong feelings of job insecurity. Inflation is under better control, except in Poland. In the governments' view, tripartite pacts with the trade unions and employers may hinder the transformation towards a more flexible labor market. The unions see themselves confronted with state measures to moderate wage increases and reduce inflation, on the one hand, and with regular spontaneous strikes, on the other.

Finally, tripartism in Western Europe is based on a tradition of bargaining at the sector level. Membership commitment was built on a voluntary base. When tripartism started, the organizational structure and the general orientation of employers and unions was one of bargaining between organizations. In Central Europe the development is almost the other way around. Tripartism shapes the organizations and imposes a kind of voluntary discipline which has not existed before. It is a "top-down" process, rather than a step towards more centralization (Héthy 1994).

NEW ISSUES AND NEW POLITICS

Labor conditions and social legislation have lost some of their importance in Western Europe. New issues have come to the fore on which labor unions and labor-based parties have been forced to focus. First is the environment. In most of Europe the idea of permanent economic growth was changed into one of "economic growth, but how?" under the influence of the oil crises and later to one questioning the need for growth at all.

Related to this change in attitude towards economic growth has been the rise of environmentalism as a major social value and political movement. The movement gained momentum in the wake of a report published in 1972 by the Club of Rome, a group of scientists and politicians, drawing attention to the implication of economic growth for the exhaustion of the earth's natural resources. The first oil crisis, which stimulated discussion on car traffic as a highly polluting form of mobility and on nuclear power, contributed to the rise of the environmental issue. Green movements, which to some extent grew out of anti-nuclear movements, sprung up, and in a number of countries even green political parties appeared. The serious accident in the Ukrainian Chernobyl power plant in 1986 aroused more widespread concern about nuclear energy and energy politics in general and contributed to the green cause. Since most of the green parties attract leftist people, they compete for votes with the traditional labor-based parties. Moreover, environmentalism challenges the labor movement's traditional emphasis on growth and higher wages. Though it is still a minor item in politics and unionism, it is on the agenda of social democratic and other parties and union congresses in most of Europe. It is also a possible cause of division between growers and ecologists. Moreover, the question has gained saliency, since growth no longer provides a solution for unemployment.

Equal rights for women has been another prominent issue since its promotion by the second feminist movement in the early 1970s. Like environmentalism, it affects social democrats and socialists more than other parties, because of the traditional links between socialism and feminism. Female action groups have pressed for equal labor conditions (a traditional ideal, but hardly ever taken very seriously) and for further reaching reforms. One of the measures advocated has been better recruitment of women for top positions in unions, parties and other social and political institutions. Most political parties have addressed the issue of women's rights but the social democrats and other socialists have been the most under attack, and most willing to respond. Imitating the example of the United States, positive action, as affirmative action is called in Europe, has become a topic of discussion and a new line of policy--not only in the labor movement but in national politics at large. Most social democratic parties have even fixed a forty percent quota for the share of women in parliament seats, and they have increased the number of women in leadership positions. Similar policies have been pursued in government agencies and public services. The issue is a much stronger one in Germanic than in Latin Europe; the communist parties of Latin Europe have never been very active in this field. Recently the quota system has come under attack, however, after a negative verdict by the European Court of Justice, a European Union institution.

A second women's demand has been a radical reduction of working hours, in order to allow men to share household tasks and women to get rid of their double workload. The goal has been a work week of less than thirty hours, but in general the women's movement has supported union demands for 35 or 36 hours --as long as they would reduce daily working time rather than lead to early retirement or longer weekends. Because female labor is concentrated in public services, public sector unions have been the first to address women's issues. In industry, the unions (and employers) have been more suspicious of changes in traditional working hours aimed at gender equality.

A third issue has been the position of immigrant workers. Many of them have become citizens of their host-countries and have acquired voting rights. The *Gastarbeiter* and their families are often concentrated in nineteenth century working-class areas in larger cities, abandoned by native workers for suburbia. These old city quarters have been the traditional strongholds of the labor-based parties, and any tension between natives who have not moved and the newcomers affects these parties in particular. Racist parties have sprung up in response to the perceived domination of city quarters by families of foreign descent and "deviant" culture. The rise of Islamic fundamentalism in the Middle East has recently fueled the resentment against the North African and the Turkish immigrants. Labor-based parties have taken a fierce stand against any new rise of racism, but they are still caught in a predicament between pressures from the older working-class population and protection of the newcomers. In the 1980s, most countries imposed checks on the stream of immigrant workers and imposed sanctions on enterprises employing illegal immigrants. An exception was Switzerland, which only allowed foreign workers, mainly from Italy, to enter into short-term contracts and sent them home at the expiration date--a kind of discrimination which was not approved of in the rest of Europe. The influx of large numbers of political fugitives from Africa, the Middle East and parts of Central and Eastern Europe in the 1990s aggravated the problem. In several countries admission policies have been tightened up--a hot issue in most social democratic and socialist parties. Germany has clung to its "open door" admission policy, but it also witnessed the most violent racist incidents in the early 1990s.

The labor-based parties and unions have entered into fierce debate on these new issues, and on other minority issues advocated by small but vociferous minorities. Environmental concerns, women's rights and the position of foreign workers are addressed at party meetings and union congresses, as well as in collective bargaining. Rather than acting as a unifying force, however, the issues have aggravated tensions between and within unions. Unions in traditional industries regard environmental priorities as a potential threat to employment. Women's rights have been easier to enforce in the public sector than in the private sector of the economy and are traded off against other gains. Moreover, work-related questions have become less important for many workers than general provisions like health care and recreational facilities for the weekend and holidays (Taylor 1993).

In sum, the union role in the social democratic parties has become less prominent. That is due not only to the rise of the new issues but also to divisions within the trade union movement and to deliberate party attempts to downplay the union role in order to attract the middle class. From a working-class stronghold, they have to some extent fallen apart into arenas of specific minorities: the women's movement, radical public sector workers, the traditional working class, moderate clerical workers and a few active immigrant workers. This growing diversity and the debate on issues other than unemployment and social security have alienated the traditional manual working class.The latter have also been disappointed by the social democrats' and socialists' involvement in cutting state spending.

Because of the changes in the economy and the labor market, cuts in budgets and the challenges to the position of the established organizations, Germanic Europe's corporatism is under stress. There are two opposing views of its future, with a lot of variation in between. The first points out that corporatism fulfills an important function in the economy. It reduces conflict, de-politicizes and legitimizes government policies, which contribute to the stability of the political system and the smooth functioning of labor relations. This explains the energetic search for this kind of tripartism in countries freed from authoritarian rule, like the Iberian Peninsula and Central Europe. Moreover, there still exists an organizational base for corporatism. The privatization of public enterprises and public services has increased the representativeness of employer associations, and in most Germanic countries over forty percent of the labor force continues to be unionized. There also continues to exist a relation of social partnership, and the organizations are able to enforce the outcome of their agreements. The differences in interests between employers and workers continue to be a basic driving force in political and social life. Social and economic issues have become even more important with the declining influence of religion, in particular that of the Catholic Church, in politics and labor relations. Protagonists of this view are mainly to be found among those involved in tripartism. They are still doing business despite the cracks in the system such as less government interest in tripartism and the rise of new confederations of clerical workers challenging the traditional confederations. They can point to the fact that even in Holland, with a unionization rate of under thirty percent, corporatism has remained viable and still influences social and economic policy. Protagonists also point to the newcomers in the field of tripartism in Latin and Central Europe.

A second view, more prevalent in the academic community, raises the question of whether corporatism is not simply a product of a certain stage of economic and political transition and is bound to disappear. Corporatism was based on the existence of a large and politically motivated labor movement trying to change the political system and society at large. However, differences in interests between employers and workers have turned into wider social and cultural cleavages, and divergences within the labor force have become almost as important, with as great a variation as the one between highly trained clerical workers in education and high-tech industries and unskilled immigrant workers in other economic sectors. Moreover, labor no longer seeks to transform the political system, and as a consequence the need for unity no longer exists or has become less urgent. Instead of a monopoly of interest organizations representing all workers (and all employers), there must be room for a plurality of interests, competing with each other for influence on the national government. This pluralist view, particularly at home in Great Britain and the United States, predicts a transition on the European continent to a plurality of worker organizations, that may combine for political reasons but will also express diverging demands. Employers will no longer be willing to impose national rules because of the rigidities they impose on the labor market and the fact that they do not suit specific conditions facing enterprises. This school of thought points to the employers' refusal to continue national bargaining in a number of Germanic countries, to be discussed in Chapter 8.

The contrast is striking. Many continentals and some Americans see European tripartism as a model to be followed, while others in Britain and the United States see it as a remnant of the past, a roundabout way of arriving at the kind of pluralism Britain and the United States had already reached in the nineteenth century. Recently, Crouch has attempted a synthesis of these ideas in a history of European labor relations. His survey does not show a development from corporatism to pluralism or vice versa. Rather, corporatism (more specific, the Germanic model) and the Latin model are stable forms of labor relations. While the stability of the Latin model is based on weak labor power, both in labor relations and in national politics, the stability of the Germanic model need not be based on trade union power, as it is in Scandinavia. Its base may also consist of an explicit and lasting government policy to grant the unions a place higher than their power and membership size merit, as in Switzerland and Holland. As a consequence, both strong and weak labor power may lead to the Germanic model. The British model (which also applies to Finland and Italy in his view) is a rather unstable one, since trade union strength is not matched with political power. As is done in this book, Crouch's idea stresses the close links between labor relations and national politics in Europe and, more specific, the relationship between the unions and the national government (Crouch 1993).

5

Collective Bargaining and Conflict

One of the features most European nations have in common, besides the close relationship between labor relations and politics, is multi-employer bargaining. Labor conditions are determined in contacts between trade unions and employers' associations, rather than in unilateral employer decision making or in contacts between trade unions and enterprise management. Because multi-employer bargaining often covers industrial sectors or branches, it is called sector bargaining or industrial branch bargaining. Here, again, there is a lot of variation both among and within nations. While in some sectors unions and employers' associations negotiate nationwide for the whole sector, in others there are only local contacts.

PRECONDITIONS FOR SECTOR BARGAINING

Why has sector bargaining become the predominant type of union-employer contact in Europe? The main precondition for its growth has been the expansion of sector trade unions for political motives, as we have seen. Employers responded to the rise of such workers' organizations by establishing their own sector associations. These activities at the sector level explain why contacts could take place at that level, but not why they took the form of bargaining. The main reason for sector contact was that the early sector unions actually were limited to skilled workers. They followed the tradition of early skilled worker unions and the craft unions by trying to impose local or even nationwide wage rates, unilaterally if possible. The early craft unions contacted all local and even the most important national employers to convince them of the need or the advantage of wage rate uniformity. By the time sector organizations had been set up, the unions contacted the employer associations. This often led to conflicts, including sector-wide strikes and lockouts. In previous times one of the organizations would have succumbed, but the socialist labor movement was determined to set up permanent organizations in all sectors, supported by the stonger unions. The result of a large conflict would then be a stalemate, for which bargaining offered a way out. Even the first national agreement, the 1899 September Agreement (*Septemberforlig*) in Denmark, was preceded by a large and long-lasting strike and a lockout. The better organized unions, like the printers' organizations, mainly organized skilled workers, and gave the example of sector wage bargaining. Unions in sectors with a large share of less skilled workers remained weakly developed and were late to enforce collective bargaining.

The main union motive to promote sector wage rates was that they took wages out of competition and provided a stable and predictable income. For that reason the unions favored formal one- or two-year agreements. In return, they would not call a strike during that period. This no-strike pledge has been part of most sector agreements from the very beginning. The unions also had a fine argument to persuade employers: Sector bargaining helps to neutralize the company from trade union activity because bargaining takes place outside and not within the company. With sector bargaining, the unions do not need to interfere with enterprise business. Labor disputes will, of course, affect individual enterprises, but they are no longer directed against the individual employers but against the employer associations. Sector bargaining shifts the arena of conflict from the workplace or the company to the sector, leaving the employer's authority intact in all matters except wages. Craft unions could not forward that argument since they wanted to have a say in the company's organization of work, fighting any change that might affect their craft. A second, less important motive for employers to comply was that sector bargaining saves time and energy, and in productive firms the result may be even better than company bargaining since it does not allow for undercutting. Without much effort of his own, the employer gets the same deal as his competitors. These advantages did not convince the employers at once. Many of them were reluctant to leave bargaining to their associations, since it reduced their own power over the enterprise.

The first sector bargaining experiments took place at the local level, but the wave of strikes at the end of World War I for the eight-hour workday forced many employers into nationwide sector bargaining--sometimes under heavy government pressure. There has been some debate as to whether the employers or the unions have determined the level of bargaining. According to Clegg, who especially focused on Britain, employers determined the level, since they were able to decide if they would hand over this competence to their association (Clegg 1976). Sisson has qualified that argument. On the continent the initiative for sector bargaining came from the unions rather than from the employers, and it was due to the unions' pressure that the level of bargaining shifted to sector bargaining. Indeed, the unions were invariably the first to get organized at the sector level. They used their organizations to press for sector wage rates or for collective bargaining. The employers determined the level of bargaining only in so far as they were able to postpone it until the moment the unions were strong enough to enforce it. In particular, large enterprise was late to accept the principle of sector bargaining because the advantages hardly applied to them. The time- and effort-saving argument was less urgent for them, and they would have to reckon with some workplace protests or union activities anyway. On the other hand, employers themselves sometimes pressed for a centralization of bargaining. In some cases they were the driving force behind national wage agreements, in particular after World War II (Sisson 1987).

Sector bargaining not only neutralizes the workplace and the enterprise, it also serves as a base for national (all-industry) bargaining. The degree of workplace neutralization, the level of bargaining and the enforcement of the outcome vary among the three models of labor relations.

COLLECTIVE BARGAINING AND CONFLICT IN THE BRITISH MODEL

Sector bargaining is least developed in Great Britain. In the British model each union negotiates with individual employers or the employer associations for its own skilled or unskilled members. The result may be multi-employer bargaining, but its outcome does not apply to the sector labor force as a whole. As a consequence, the diversity in bargaining patterns and outcomes is greater than on the continent. A number of conditions reinforce this diversity. Multi-employer bargaining has always focused on procedural rules as much as on substantive labor conditions, leaving most of the latter to union-management contacts within the enterprise. The procedures help to solve conflicts that arise from enterprise bargaining but leave intact the position of the company or the workplace as the major bargaining level. Bargaining within the enterprise takes place almost continuously and in an informal way between the rather autonomous union shop stewards and various levels of management. It covers both general labor conditions, like wages and working time, and specific working conditions, like the introduction of new technologies and changes in work organization. This means that the neutralization of the enterprise and the workplace is only partial, in contrast to sector bargaining. The craft unions fight any change in the division of work that would undermine their craft as an attack against their position. Moreover, diversity is greater than on the continent because collective bargaining has hardly been subject to legislation--in line with the insulation of labor relations from politics. Governments have supported collective bargaining in an indirect way, by promoting it in the public sector, for instance, and by promoting joint employer-union "Wage Councils" in unorganized trades.

In the 1960s this type of decentralized bargaining, not only for wage rates and working time but also for the division of work within the enterprise, was increasingly considered to hamper the introduction of advanced production processes and new work patterns. In its 1968 report, the Donovan Commission, established to provide a cure, called British labor relations largely informal and fragmented and advocated the integration of multi-employer and workplace bargaining and the formalization of bargaining at company level. A move in that direction followed, but so did a large decline in multi-employer bargaining and an increase in unilateral management decision making in labor conditions without any union involvement (the "non-union firms"). British collective bargaining has remained highly decentralized, and so has collective conflict. Like bargaining, labor conflict can start any moment, and the decision is made at the workplace. Strikes are small and short, but very numerous. To some extent the same model applies to Ireland. That country has imitated the British system of workplace and enterprise bargaining, albeit it with regular attempts at peak-level bargaining. Both Great Britain and Ireland are strike-prone countries, surpassed only by Italy and Spain in working hours spent on strike. The British and Irish position clearly shows that the strike rate is not a matter of "southern" or "Mediterranean" temperament, but one of labor relations system.

COLLECTIVE BARGAINING AND CONFLICT IN GERMANIC EUROPE

In Germanic Europe, each of the sector organizations negotiates at least a dozen sector and branch agreements, ranging from very large ones in the machine industry to smaller agreements covering umbrella manufacturing or dental assistants. With a few exceptions, manual and clerical workers are covered by separate agreements. Sector bargaining takes place annually or every other year, usually during the winter months. Where unions belonging to different confederations (social democratic, Catholic) take part in the negotiations, the lists of demands are often coordinated in advance. The negotiations result in a written agreement, which is binding upon both sides and includes a social peace or labor peace clause, that limits labor conflicts to the period of bargaining and bans them during the rest of the year. Collective bargaining not only neutralizes the company, it pacifies the whole sector during the term of the agreement. In Scandinavia the labor market parties make a distinction between "conflicts of interest" and "conflicts of rights." The former refer to a dispute about the terms of a new agreement, which may result in a strike. Conflicts of rights concern the interpretation of agreements. Strikes over rights are not allowed, and the dispute will be solved by the sector organizations or by joint union-employer labor courts in case the mediation procedure fails at the sector level. A similar distinction is made in the other Germanic countries.

In most of the smaller nations negotiations cover the whole sector, nationwide. Only in Germany are almost all agreements (*Tarif, Tarifvertrag*) concluded for each federal state (*Land*) separately or for important industrial regions within a federal state, but the negotiations are heavily coordinated by the national sector organizations. In all nations the annual rounds of collective bargaining are subject to two forms of coordination. First, the peak organizations coordinate sector demands. This kind of coordination is stronger in the smaller nations than in Germany. The second form of coordination consists of "pattern bargaining," in which leading sectors set the pattern for others. The dominant position of IG Metall in Germany allows it to set the tone for the other sectors. In the smaller countries, the metalworkers' unions also tend to play this role of trendsetter but within a stricter national framework. Agreements between IG Metall and the employers' association Gesamtmetall not only serve as pilot agreements for the rest of the German economy but also have an impact on the smaller nations. They are the only foreign collective wage negotiations that make headlines in all of these countries.

The core of this system of sector bargaining is the compliance it imposes upon individual employers and union members. The idea is to create a web of sector or branch agreements into which all companies fit. Consequently, "non-union firms," which refuse any form of collective bargaining, hardly exist in the Germanic model, in contrast to the British model. After all, firms do not need to bargain since they will be covered by the sector agreement. The predominance of sector bargaining does not exclude enterprise bargaining. Indeed, in the smaller countries the great majority of employees are covered by sector agreements, but there are far more enterprise agreements than sector agreements. In Holland the 200 nationwide sector agreements cover over 2.5 million workers and the 700 company agreements 0.5 million. The 500 nationwide and regional sector agreements in Switzerland cover 1,250,000 workers, while the more than 600 enterprise agreements cover only 150,000. The enterprise agreements have different backgrounds. Sometimes they go back to the 1920s or 1930s, when large enterprises finally gave up their opposition to bargaining and concluded company agreements. The sheer size of a company may also provide a motive to conclude enterprise agreements rather than join the sector agreement. Other reasons for enterprise agreements are that the enterprise is part of a sector in which employers are hardly organized or falls between two sectors. Sometimes employers want to conclude an enterprise agreement because they oppose the employer associations' concessions, or because they are more willing to compromise. Such "black raven" or "white doves," depending upon their considerations, then have to give up membership in the employers' associations, if they are not kicked out before. Such firms are a rather marginal phenomenon, however. Germany is strictest in its application of the sector principle. The only major company to engage in enterprise bargaining is Volkswagen, due to the fact that this company is partly under public control and is not affiliated with an employers' association.

Enterprise bargaining does not really undermine sector bargaining as the leading principle in the Germanic model. Not only do sector agreements cover far more workers than do enterprise agreements, more important is that enterprise negotiations are done by sector union officials in cooperation with representatives from the workforce, rather than by the latter alone. Moreover, the negotiations take place within a framework of sector demands listed by the unions and of sector priorities, which are discussed within employer organizations. What is negotiated is not so much an enterprise-specific list of points as an enterprise-adapted sector list. However, in enterprises that conform to sector agreements bargaining may take place between union representatives and management, supplementary to sector bargaining. Here, there is some room for additional and enterprise-specific demands, and for experiments with new labor conditions before they become part of the sector list of demands. In particular, large companies in the machine industry serve that purpose, as with Volkswagen in Germany. Still, this bargaining has to comply with the peace obligation laid down in the sector or enterprise agreement (Streeck 1984; Thelen 1992).

In accordance with the peace clause and the distinction between conflicts of interest and conflicts of rights, strikes tend to be well organized and announced in advance to the employers. Most unions possess large strike funds, which are rarely used, however. In most of these countries strikes are exceptional interruptions of normal life. Strikes during the term of an agreement are rare, but sporadic wildcat strikes that are not supported by the trade unions occur. Finland, with a shorter bargaining tradition and more wildcat action, and Belgium, especially its French speaking part, have the highest strike rates in Germanic Europe. In Austria and Switzerland there are hardly any strikes at all. Only in Germany do lockouts also belong to the labor relations armory stock. In Scandinavia they are very rare and in the other countries there have not been any lockouts in the second half of this century. In most nations there exist voluntary mediation procedures or institutions, set up by unions and employers associations themselves.

Due to the strong bargaining tradition, the national government remains on the sidelines, fulfilling two supportive functions. First, it provides a legal framework for collective bargaining and conflict. This function is less developed in Scandinavia, where the parties have laid down their own rules in the Basic Agreements. Belgian law provides for specific joint ("parity") committees for sector bargaining, consisting of small union and employer delegations and chaired by an independent mediator. There exist a couple of dozen of such commitees, most of them covering either manual or clerical workers in the various branches. However, bargaining often takes place in a more informal setting outside the committee, in which case the committee is used only to get the final and official text of the agreement into the minutes.

Conflict legislation is also less extensive in Scandinavia, but the rules are similar in most countries. Strikes are allowed only in case of conflicts of interest, to use the Scandinavian term. If a strike is called (a number of countries require a seventy-five percent majority vote in favor), employers may appeal either to a labor court or to a regular court. The court will base its judgment about the legality of the action on arguments of timing and of proportionality. Has due procedure for bargaining been followed, and has the strike not been called in a too-early stage of the procedure? Is the action excessive compared to the issue at hand, or stated in more general terms, does the goal justify the means? The judgement is often a surprise, and in Germany and Holland organizations eagerly, and nervously, await it each time a court decision is necessary. In Germany rules on lockouts have been a major bone of contention between employers and unions. On several occasions one side has appealed to the Constitutional Court to reaffirm the right to call a lockout (*Aussperrung*) or to prevent one.

The second government function is to legally extend the application of collective agreements to unorganized employers. Legal extension is hardly ever an issue, since both unions and employers are in favor. It mainly serves to bring dissenting companies in line. In Belgium, the joint committees mainly derive their importance to bargaining from the fact that only agreements concluded in a committee can be legally extended. However, legal extension is more important in countries with a lower union density and less union power to enforce compliance. The Dutch unions would probably be the only ones to run into trouble if legal extension did not exist.

To summarize, collective bargaining in Germanic Europe is characterized by two basic features. First, it neutralizes the workplace by enforcing compliance with sector bargaining results, whatever the outcome. Second, the position of the national government is a supportive one and hardly contested. The tradition of bargaining has shaped a relationship of mutual trust over the years. It is expressed in terms like *Tarifpartner* in Germany and *sociale partners* in Holland and Belgium. The Scandinavians don't like such cozy words; they stick to the term "labor market parties" for unions and employers' associations.

COLLECTIVE BARGAINING AND CONFLICT IN LATIN EUROPE

Collective bargaining in Latin Europe also covers sectors rather than enterprises, but local and regional bargaining predominates. There are two reasons for the choice of local instead of nationwide sector bargaining. Both of them have to do with employers' preferences--which lends some support to Clegg's thesis that employers rather than unions have decided at which level collective bargaining will take place. First, employers' organizations are only loosely organized, leaving much freedom to individual employers. Local bargaining provides individual employers an opportunity to become intimately involved in the preparation of the negotiations and in the process itself. The second reason refers to the role of government. The mutual distrust between unions and employers is greater than in the Germanic model and is expressed in common language. In Latin Europe, the rather neutral term employer is hardly used. Unions and employers prefer the term *patron* and *patronat*, which suggest more distance, between "them" and "us." The distance between the two sides has made the unions direct themselves to the national government in order to add weight to their demands. A call for a nationwide strike to put pressure on the government mobilizes more members and non-members alike and has a larger impact than a local sector strike. Therefore, employers prefer to bargain on a local base. Of course, some coordination takes place on both sides by the national sector organizations, but the main thrust of bargaining is regional and the differences in labor conditions are larger than in Germany (except those between the recently reunified parts of Germany).

Italy has the strongest tradition of nationwide sector bargaining in Latin Europe, but most of the time the agreements concluded at that level have mainly served as the starting point of local and enterprise bargaining, without much impact on these negotiations. Moreover, the number of Italian nationwide agreements is very limited, less than twenty. One single agreement applies to the car industry, several other branches of the machine industry, steel works, shipyards and the electrotechnical industry--all at the same time. This broad coverage does not allow the agreements to take into consideration regional and branch differences and increases the need for further regional and branch bargaining. In Spain, the federalization of the country has stimulated the regionalization of bargaining.

Due to the direct link between labor relations and national politics the government is more involved than in the Germanic model. It stands just outside the door of the bargaining room, but the unions always look for an opportunity to open the door, because they (rightly) believe that the employers are not really interested in collective bargaining. The national government also exercises the same two functions it has in the Germanic model: providing a legal framework for collective bargaining and extending the application of agreements. The latter is rather undisputed, since the local employers have had a chance to influence the bargaining process. The former is affected by the process of politicization. Rather than sanction existing bargaining practice, it serves to restart collective bargaining when it has been given up.

Collective bargaining in the Latin model is regularly in need of an impetus to bring the two parties to the bargaining table again. In the 1980s governments in France, Italy and Portugal used the public sector to introduce new forms of collective bargaining or to stimulate bargaining in the rest of the economy. Sometimes this government exhortation, especially when directed towards employers, is exercised under union pressure or the pressure of a large strike movement. Invariably the result is short-lived, which is not surprising, since a partisan force that may be called in by the unions to enforce bargaining demands is not the right agency to encourage employers to negotiate. Employers tend to see the second activity as a mere variation of the first one, imposing something upon them under union pressure. Consequently, legislation on collective bargaining does not have much impact on the process of bargaining. In contrast to France, which has some fine pieces of legislation on collective bargaining, Italian governments have tried to stimulate bargaining without recourse to the law. Actually, Italy does not have such legislation at all. Formally, collective agreements in that country apply to trade union members only, not to unorganized workers, but in practice the latter enjoy the same labor conditions.

In addition to the position of the national government, the second difference with Germanic bargaining is that labor peace is much less of a sacred principle. The distinction between conflicts of interest and conflicts of rights applies only to a limited extent. In the Germanic model new negotiations start some time before the expiration date of the existing agreement, while in Latin Europe the current agreement is supposed to be expiring when new negotiations start or when a strike is called. Collective agreements may contain a no-strike clause, but unions are not willing to enforce it since the notion of enforcing compliance is contrary to their very nature. The effect is that collective bargaining does not set strict limits to enterprise bargaining or curtail worker action within the enterprise. In Italy, anything may be negotiated at any level, almost without reference to previous bargaining. In practice, enterprise bargaining in the larger Italian enterprises precedes industry bargaining in the sector involved and determines its outcome, rather than the other way around.

This autonomy of enterprise bargaining is an offshoot of the relations between the trade unions. In the Germanic model either one union may be involved or a few, which are often in close cooperation. In Latin Europe at least two unions participate. They may cooperate at times, but one of them (mostly the communist-dominated one) may refuse to bargain at all, leave the bargaining table during the negotiations, or refuse to sign the agreement and then try to undermine it or undo it through enterprise bargaining. As a consequence, the enterprise remains an arena of conflict.

The differences between the Germanic and the Latin types of sector bargaining have been exaggerated here. They are certainly not as pronounced as in the link between labor relations and politics, discussed in the previous chapters. The comparison is complicated by the fact that the Latin model covers only a few countries, in two of which (the Iberian Peninsula) collective bargaining did not start until recently. Moreover, national variations are larger than in the Germanic model, since bargaining is more decentralized and conflict plays a greater role. Italy is the most strike-prone country in Europe, followed by Spain. Characterizing the French experience is difficult. At times, France has had high strike rates, but they have gone down since the 1970s and in the last years private sector strikes have been rare. The membership decrease in the French unions has been offered as an explanation for this downward tendency in overt conflict. It has also caused a change in the strike pattern, from larger actions-- spontaneously started but extended by the trade unions--to small and more isolated work stoppages, with no mutual link.

In sum, continental bargaining differs from the British model in the degree of government involvement (in the form of sanctioning or stimulating bargaining and extending bargaining results) and in the shift in conflict level from the enterprise to the sector level. In Latin Europe government involvement is stronger and the shift less effective than in the Germanic model.

NATIONAL BARGAINING

On the European continent the umbrella organizations coordinate collective
bargaining demands on both sides. Collective wage bargaining by the peak
organizations themselves is less common. Only in Scandinavia have national
wage negotiations formed an integral part of labor relations. In Sweden it has
been the major type of bargaining since 1956, in Norway it has alternated with
sector bargaining, and in Denmark it took place in the 1960s and 1970s
(Calmfors 1990). The other small Germanic countries have had shorter periods
of peak-level wage bargaining. In the large countries and in Latin Europe
national wage negotiations have been just as or even more exceptional than
tripartite meetings with the national government. Only in Italy has it been
practiced more than once.

Depending on the economic or labor market conditions either the employers,
the unions, or the national governments have been the driving force behind
national wage bargaining. In the 1950s and 1960s, under conditions of full
employment and strong economic growth, employers favored centralization. In
national negotiations, the employers expected that the unions would also take into
account the conditions of less prospering sectors. This employer argument was
the driving force behind the start of national wage bargaining in Sweden in 1956.
While the employers used this kind of bargaining to "level down" wage increases
to those that less productive or less sheltered sectors could afford, the unions
aimed at a "leveling up" in the poorer paying sectors. This quest for more
equality was most pronounced in the "solidaristic wage policy" of the Swedish
trade unions, the staunchest advocates of centralization among the European
unions.

Under national bargaining the leading sectors have to accept some degree of
moderation, while others are the main beneficiaries. This may easily lead to
tensions within both the union and employers' confederations between the well-
paid or well-paying sectors and the other member organizations. In a comparative
study of bargaining in Sweden and Germany, Swenson has even shown that it led
to coalitions between union and employer factions. In Sweden such a
combination existed in the 1920s, when an alliance of metalworkers and other
unions and employers tried to curb the highly paid construction workers.
Recently such a union-employer combination was directed against the
metalworkers, by that time the best-paid manual workers. The metalworkers
defected from the system of peak-level bargaining on their own initiative since
they were more interested in leveling-up in comparison with clerical workers,
most of whom were organized in separate organizations of their own and covered
by separate agreements. In Germany such a union-employer coalition against IG
Metall failed (Swenson 1985).

Since the mid-1970s most national wage bargaining has been due to
government pressure. The overriding argument has been wage restraint, pressing
both sides to take into account the conditions of less competitive sectors.

Centralized bargaining provides the national government with a better opportunity to monitor the negotiations or at least to exercise some influence because of its contacts with the peak organizations, especially in the corporatist countries. Rather than a series of central agreements, the result has often consisted of one or two incidental agreements between two or three parties. They vary from vague declarations of intent to strict wage limits for the member organizations. In the former case sector bargaining is left intact, and the member organizations may neglect the serious warnings or recommendations. In the latter case, sector bargaining is confined to the elaboration of the wage increase allowed by the national agreement.

The absence of a longer series of peak-level agreements in the 1980s and 1990s has been due to all three parties. National governments still urge such agreements, but they have nothing to offer in compensation for wage restraint except severe cuts in the state budget. Employers have become increasingly hostile towards national wage agreements, since the latter do not lead to wage moderation and fail to take into account enterprise-specific conditions. In some countries, including Sweden, employers have announced their determination not to participate in any new peak bargaining. Unions complain about their own weakening position among their members in view of the lack of compensation for wage restraint.

Outside the smaller Germanic (corporatist) nations, national wage bargaining has been most common in Ireland, a clear deviation from its British model characteristics. Its history shows the changes over time. In the 1960s union and employer efforts to promote centralization proved abortive, and led to, if anything at all, a rise in strikes. In 1970 the Irish government threatened to impose statutory wage and price controls, which prompted some form of mutual understanding between the peak organizations. In the 1970s a number of "National Wages Agreements" were concluded, fixing the wage increases for the entire dependent labor force. In 1973 the oil crisis interfered, and the agreements met with the same problems as peak-level bargaining had in Belgium and Denmark: wage drift and union complaints about tied hands. The national government then became involved in a direct way. At the end of the 1970s the Agreements were replaced by a three-party "National Understanding," which merely served as a last chance to escape statutory wage controls. After two such Understandings the efforts to coordinate bargaining in that way were given up.

STATUTORY WAGE POLICIES

The Irish experience shows that three-party talks in the 1980s and 1990s have sometimes been a form of government intervention in disguise. This is not a new development; peak-level bargaining and state wage policies have been related since World War II. Both are confined to the continent. Great Britain's only example of statutory wage policies was in the mid-1960s, right after the conclusion of the "Social Contract" between the Labour Party and the unions, and both failed due to the prevalence of decentralized bargaining.

On the continent, wage policies can be traced back to the end of World War II, when the need for postwar reconstruction in combination with scarcity urged most governments to impose ceilings upon wages, sometimes in combination with a statutory minimum wage and a legal regulation of the work week. The only two countries without any wage policies were Sweden and Switzerland, neither of which was involved in the war. In most countries this kind of wage regulation ended in the early 1950s. By that time legal or other provisions had been framed for collective bargaining or conflict resolution. However, the introduction of Keynesian economic policies provided in particular the national confederations in the corporatist countries with a motive to remain involved in wage bargaining, and the national government with a good reason to advise on the proper wage increase (Flanagan, Soskice, Ulman 1983). The Austrian *Sozialpartner*, represented in the joint *Paritätische Kommission*, monitored the bargaining results in close contact with government ministers. Holland had the most extensive and strictest wage policy, lasting until the mid-1960s. In this "guided wage policy" all sector agreements were subject to government approval, with the confederations heavily involved in setting the guidelines and checking to ensure that the agreements complied with them.

In the 1960s the tight labor market in Europe gave rise to large wage increases. Governments tried to curb inflation by pressing for more central coordination of wage bargaining, like the German *Konzertierte Aktion*. One of the means to curb inflation was to link wage increase to productivity growth and rises in price levels, a formula which was generally accepted in the 1960s. After the 1974 oil crisis inflation prompted unions to increase wage demands, and national governments tried once again to step in. Since that time all European governments have at times interfered in wage bargaining, Switzerland and Germany being the only exceptions. The legally sanctioned autonomy of the parties (*Tarifautonomie*) in Germany does not allow for direct state intervention in collective bargaining.

State intervention since the oil crisis has taken various forms. Intervention has ranged from friendly recommendations to compulsory measures, and from urgent advice to take into account the rate of unemployment to threats to "adapt" employment policies. The most stringent form consists of compulsory guidelines issued before the start of a bargaining round, leaving the organizations no other option than to comply and confine bargaining to the elaboration of the allowed increase. The Belgian government used this instrument in the early 1980s. A second form consists of government efforts to interfere in the bargaining process in case the negotiations seem to result in conflict or the sector organizations do not comply with peak-level recommendations or rules. In the former case, compulsory arbitration may be imposed. The latter is found in Denmark, where the government has extended the national agreements to deviant sectors. Even when collective bargaining is completed, governments have at their disposal the means to interfere. This interference is, of course, more effective if announced in advance. An example is a change in taxes, effectively taxing away any wage increase. A highly explosive policy instrument has been intervention in wage indexation, the automatic adaptation of wages to prices during the term of an agreement. In Italy and Belgium, where this indexation is a sacred principle, governments have made it inoperative more than once in the 1980s and 1990s, in the face of strong union opposition.

Compulsory measures have become increasingly unpopular, however, because they lead to union protest and to increasing union efforts to compensate for the restraint in the following bargaining rounds. This follow-up has raised serious doubts about the positive effect of any compulsory guidelines. They might even have an adverse effect due to "overcompensation" in the years following the wage freeze or wage pause. A second reason has been that, especially in the Germanic model, the national government became a target of action. Government intervention contributed to a politicization of labor relations, which placed a strain on other state policies. Additional pressures against compulsory wage restraint have been the general trend towards deregulation in the 1980s, encouraged by the national governments, and the fact that governments are unwilling to offer anything in return for wage restraint. Consequently the strict wage policies of the late 1970s and early 1980s have been abandoned in favor of less direct government intervention (Michels and Slomp 1990). A popular means to that end has been the use of the public sector as a kind of wage restraint model for the rest of the economy.

THE PUBLIC SECTOR

The public sector is comprised of two distinct parts. In the first are nationalized industries and enterprises, for example in coal mining, the steel industry, energy (especially in Italy) and also car manufacturing, like Renault in France. Nationalization of such key industries had been a long-standing demand of social democrats and communists alike. It took place mostly immediately following World War II, either because the former enterprise owners had supported the fascist cause (France), or because they lacked financial means for investment (Great Britain). In both countries this part of the public sector has periodically expanded and contracted, with nationalization interchanging with privatization depending on government composition. In Italy and Austria public enterprise has been a more stable force in the economy and in labor relations. In Germany its size has always been small, due to the Allied opposition against nationalization after the war.

Nationalized enterprises (and in some countries also the national railway company and the postal services) have played an important role in labor relations. Because of their high unionization rate, nationalized enterprises have even acted as pilot enterprises or sectors, setting the pace for other industries and introducing innovations in labor conditions--in particular in Latin Europe, with its large public sector.

The second part of the public sector consists of public services that are financed or subsidized by the state, like education, health care and social work. In contrast to the nationalized industries, these services lack a profit orientation, and productivity is difficult to measure. Until the 1960s hardly anyone interested in labor relations paid attention to the public services. Most public employees then were in a privileged position, with job security or even "tenure." The lack of formal bargaining rights or procedures provided the only disadvantage these workers faced. Collective bargaining with state employees was rejected on grounds that it would affect state authority and sovereignty. For the most part, governments mandated labor conditions in this sector, after consultation with the public sector unions. The main yardstick used for wage increases was the average wage increase in the private sector. The public services thus followed the trends in the private sector, with appropriate adaptation (Treu 1987).

The enormous expansion of public services in the 1960s and 1970s made this part of the public sector a core activity in the national economy, mainly employing clerical workers and with a large female labor force. Increasingly, however, the trade unions in the public services demanded "real" collective bargaining, including the right to strike. Governments gave in and specific government agencies came to act as "employers," but the bargaining results remained subject to government approval. The right to strike was a more hotly debated issue than collective bargaining, since governments feared strikes by workers in a monopoly position in public transport and public utilities. The right was often granted and sometimes even extended to firemen and policemen--with guarantees for public order, of course. A major exception to this pattern is the German *Beamte*, who make up only a part of the German civil service and public services. They have "tenure" status and the right to unionize, but not the right to strike or the right of collective bargaining.

However, collective bargaining in the public sector also had a positive side for national governments. Under pressure from increasing budget deficits and the unpopularity of new taxes governments were able to enforce wage restraint in the public sector. They could do so independently from the bargaining outcome in the private sector, since the public services no longer merely followed the trends in the private sector. In addition, wage restraint in the public sector came to serve as an example for the rest of the economy. In most countries the public sector changed from a position of trendfollower to one of trendsetter, and was used by the government to set a pattern in wage restraint--in the expectation that the private sector unions would not allow a gap between public and private sector wages and would follow this example.

This form of wage restraint, in combination with cuts in the budget which increased the workload, gave rise to workers' actions in education and in health care. In the 1980s such public sector strikes made up a sizable portion of all labor disputes. They were paid much attention to, particularly because categories of workers who up until this point had not been very strike prone, like nurses, participated in the actions. One of the larger strikes in the smaller Germanic nations was a combined action by Swedish clerical workers and public sector workers in 1980, the largest Swedish labor dispute in decades. Such conflicts have affected the government's position in the Germanic model. Although a distinction is to be made between political strikes as such and public sector strikes directed aginst the government as employer, the latter has contributed to a politicization of labor relations. The partial shift of conflict from the private to the public sector has reduced the difference between the German and the Latin model, since it places the government in the forefront of labor relations and in a disputed position.

In the 1990s the public sector lost some of its importance in labor relations. Public enterprises and services have been privatized by conservative governments, in particular in France and Great Britain, or they have been reduced in size (Ferner 1994). At the same time, national governments have to some extent returned to their previous position with respect to public sector bargaining --one of "real" bargaining, taking into account not only budget deficits but also pay increases in the private sector.

6

Worker Participation in the Enterprise

Since the late 1960s worker participation in enterprise decision making has been a popular topic in labor relations literature. Works councils and other devices for worker participation figure in all discussions of new trends in European labor relations. This chapter compares participation rules and participation practices in Europe and examines their place in labor relations. After a short historical note, the discussion starts with works councils, often regarded as the "real" institution of worker participation.

A SHORT HISTORY

The early craft unions often had workplace representation in the form of trade union shop stewards. On the continent, democracy within the enterprise has been a long-standing social democratic and socialist ideal, but in practice it was often downplayed in favor of collective bargaining. Only at times of great upheaval did the unions focus upon it. An example was the wave of spontaneous strikes at the end of World War I, which led to the legal recognition of works councils in Austria and Germany (crushed by the Nazi regime) and the demand of labor force representation put forward at the 1936 Matignon Agreement in France.

The existing forms of worker participation mainly date from 1945. The major reason for their introduction was the need for postwar reconstruction, which was to be a common effort not to be disrupted by management-union conflicts. Especially in countries where many employers had supported the fascist cause, as in Germany and France, worker supervision of enterprise policy provided a second motive to create some form of worker participation in enterprise decision making, as a weaker alternative to outright nationalization. In Germany, the unions advocated co-determination for that reason--that is, worker representation on the managerial board and the supervisory board of large companies. Co-determination became a very hot issue right after the foundation of the German Federal Republic, especially under the influence of the Cold War. Trade unionists pointed to the activities of large enterprises in war mongering and even in the Holocaust, which raised the need for more industrial democracy. Employers stressed the freedom of enterprise and of property as basic human rights, which would be undermined by the reintroduction of co-determination.

In the late 1950s and the 1960s, union priority was with collective bargaining rather than with works councils. Worker participation did not play an important role in labor relations, because of the focus on productivity growth and the centralization of bargaining. It was not until the May 1968 revolt in Paris with its slogan of self-management (*autogestion*) that worker participation aroused new interest. The unions changed their focus to the negative effects of continuous restructuring, increasing workload and labor mobility on the workers' social life, rather than simply their positive effects on wages. An international participation offensive was unleashed to fight worker alienation, another new term in the 1968 revolt. Since the demand was for radical change and governments were more willing to lend an ear than employers, the unions turned to politics, even in Scandinavia. A wave of legislation reinforced works council rights and worker participation in general. The Swedish unions pioneered far-reaching forms of worker involvement in decision making, which reached its height in the 1976 Worker Participation Act (*Medbestämmandelagen*, MBL). In several countries joint or other committees studied the advantages and disadvantages of co-determination, like the Bullock Committee in Britain and the Sudreau Committee in France.

In the 1980s the union offensive changed to defensive action in response to the increasing speed with which new technologies were introduced and to the spread of new forms of management-initiated worker involvement in workplace decisions. Unions and works councils shifted their attention to the employment effects of new technology. In a number of countries "technology agreements" were concluded, obliging management to inform the unions or the works council about the introduction of new technologies. A major problem, however, consisted of the growing internationalization of the national economies, which allowed management to hide behind decisions made at company headquarters, often outside the country. Rising unemployment did not favor worker participation either (IDE 1993). The European Union has engaged in efforts to set information and participation rules for multinational enterprises, resulting in the first "European works councils" in the 1990s, discussed in Chapter 9.

WORKS COUNCILS

Works councils have existed for a long period of time in a number of Germanic countries. An exception is Sweden where they existed until the participation offensive in the 1970s, when the unions turned their backs on the councils in favor of trade union representation--a logical step, as we shall see. Works councils also exist in Latin Europe, but the only country in which they have a longer history is France, where the *comité d'entreprise* was introduced in 1945. In the British model works councils are very rare because the unions refuse any "rival" institution which could challenge their position in the workplace--their main level of activity (Slomp 1995).

The introduction and the contents of the national rules on works councils reflect differences in labor relations and in legal traditions. In Scandinavia they are not covered by law but by a "Cooperation Agreement," in line with the Scandinavian preference for union-employer self-rule. This also applied to the Swedish works councils, but the 1976 extension of worker participation was introduced by law after failed union attempts to enforce it in a national agreement.

In all other nations works councils are covered by law. To some extent legislation reflects differences in models of labor relations. In France, the introduction of works councils in 1945, right after the war, was an accomplishment of the postwar socialist-communist domination of government. In the Germanic countries there was more of a debate, sometimes even a fierce one, in particular about the works councils' right to check information provided by management. In general, works councils were not a very contentious issue, however. In Germany their introduction was overshadowed by the debate on co-determination at the board level.

Works council legislation and agreements reveal a number of interesting differences. The minimum size of enterprises which are (legally) obligated to set up a council ranges from five employees in Germany to one hundred. More common is a limit of thirty-five or fifty. Where that limit applies, one of the major topics of discussion in the 1980s has been the extension of this form of worker participation to small enterprises. The problems the unions face in that segment of the economy--in the form of worker acquiescence and reluctance, as well as informal employer influence, are shown by the lack of works councils in the smaller German enterprises. Despite the obligation to establish councils in all enterprises with five or more employees, hardly any councils exist in the smaller enterprises. (In the smallest enterprises the council would actually consist of only one employee.) This absence forms part of a more general relation between enterprise size and compliance with the obligation. While most large enterprises do have works councils, in the smaller ones the unions often find it difficult to recruit potential members.

There are three variations in council composition. The first one is a joint employee-management council, prevailing in Belgium and Denmark. Since management is represented by a number of people, this composition may lead to rather arbitrary management decisions with respect to who is considered a managerial employee. Such employees then participate on the employers' side and are not eligible for election on the employees' side. The second type of council consists of employees, with the general manager presiding over the meetings, the form prevalent in France. In both cases the council is a meeting place between employees and management. The third type of council consist of employees only. In this case the council is autonomous from the employer, and its meetings, without management, are distinct from the common meetings with enterprise managers. This form exists in Germany and Austria. Holland later followed their example when it shifted from the "manager-presided" to the "autonomous" type in 1979.

The relationship between the works councils and the trade unions is a very close one. In some countries the unions enjoy a nomination monopoly, and as a consequence only organized workers make up the works councils. In other countries groups of unorganized workers have a right to nominate candidates. Elections are held every two to four years and the average turnout is seventy percent or more, which is not much higher than in local or national politics. Where more unions compete for votes, the elections are a real popularity contest, similar to local elections. The French and Spanish elections are also used to measure the support for the trade unions, since the membership data provided by the unions are unreliable. In Germany they constitute a popularity poll for the dominant DGB.

In almost all nations organized workers occupy a majority of the seats. However, in France, the CGT--which used to get the most votes, though still a minority--has lost that position to the non-unionized workers, who now make up the largest single category. Council members enjoy legal or other protection against arbitrary management action, and firing them often requires a long judicial or other procedure. They are also exempted from work for a number of hours. In some countries one or more council members may even devote all their working time to council activities. The larger German companies may have more than a dozen such full-time council members.

In general, the councils possess three kinds of rights. Without exception, the first right is to be informed about the general conditions and prospects of the enterprise: the right of information. This is clearly demonstrated in one of the latest legal documents, the Spanish Workers' Statute (*Estatuto de los Trabajadores*), in which the list of competencies opens with: "1.1. *Recibir información....*" Most legal or other rules prescribe the amount of information to be supplied on a quarterly or annual base, as well as the information to be forwarded before a decision is made in a specific field. In France the kind of periodic reports to be presented is prescribed in great detail. They include quarterly data on the size of the order file, production schedules, employment figures and likely changes in capital goods and production methods that could affect working conditions. Other countries focus less on the precise nature of the information and more on the kind of decisions about which the works council has to be informed in advance.

The second right in all countries is one of consultation in economic and financial matters. This right is often combined with the first one. Management provides information about the "state of the enterprise," followed by a discussion of the economic prospects and specific economic themes. Even the combination of the first two rights is less important, however, than the third right--the right of consent in social and personnel affairs. This may even amount to a veto right, to be overruled only by a decision of a joint union-employer arbitration committee, or by a labor court ruling. Personnel affairs subject to this right of consent are rules pertaining to employment, the hiring and dismissal of workers and on-the-job training. Social affairs include work schedules, holiday schedules, health and safety and social benefits, in addition to legal or other rights.

Works councils are also entitled to check enterprise compliance with social legislation and with collective agreements. They are not permitted to change such agreements or, more generally, to deal with labor conditions negotiated between unions and employers. They may, however, work them out in detail, which allows some freedom of interpretation. In Germany, where sector bargaining is a more sacred principle than in the other countries, this elaboration has greater importance. It takes the form of a company agreement (*Betriebsvereinbarung*). These social and personnel matters are the topics unions and works council representatives are really interested in. Most of all, they are concerned with the employment prospects. Whatever the subject at hand, the effects on employment will be discussed first and foremost. The national technology agreements of the early 1980s extended the right of information and consultation before and during the introduction of new technologies that would affect labor. A more recent development has been the extension of information and participation rights in environmental policies.

In large companies with more than one subsidiary and with a number of plants, there often exists a works council in each plant and each subsidiary or company division, as well as a peak-level concern works council, consisting of representatives from the plant or division works councils. They especially play a role in the larger German companies. The total number of councils in the largest concerns may even exceed one hundred.

TRADE UNION REPRESENTATION WITHIN THE ENTERPRISE

All European unions have their own representation in the enterprise, in the form of the British shop stewards, the French *délégues syndicaux* and *sections syndicales* and the German *Vertrauensleute* ("confidential men"). In most countries this kind of representation is covered by national or sector agreements, rather than by law. The argument is that the law can impose a labor force representation in the form of the works council, but not a union representation. A more practical argument is that if the unions are unable to enforce such a representation by themselves, they will also be too weak to enforce compliance with the law. This does not apply to France, where union representation was one of the subjects of the 1968 Constat de Grenelle and was later covered by law.

Because of the absence of legal rules and the fact that representation reflects union interest in grassroots activities and union power, there are wide variations in the nature and the activities of union representatives between nations, between sectors, and even within sectors. In most countries the union delegates are elected by the union members within the enterprise, or for each workplace separately. Trade union organizations monitor the delegate elections, but their influence is rather limited since the number of union militants prepared to act as delegates is limited. Due to the absence of legal rules, the delegates have less recourse to legal action in the case of arbitrary employer action, but joint union-employer committees often act as a court of appeal. Moreover, in the countries where works councils exist, most delegates will be council members and enjoy the legal or other rights the membership entails. Like works council members, union representatives may be exempted from work for their union activities, and most large enterprises have a number of full-time union delegates.

The British shop stewards probably enjoy the highest degree of autonomy from their unions, and only in the British model do shop stewards make up the core of trade union activities. Since the 1960s British shop stewards have almost supplanted union leaders as the main actors in bargaining. Recent employer efforts at unilateral decision making, without collective bargaining, have reinforced that position, leaving the shop stewards as the last instance of union influence in managerial decision making. Even in enterprises with union recognition agreements, employers have attempted to reduce the unions' role in labor condition decisions, often without formally putting an end to this recognition. However, examples of "de-recognition" have received wide publicity, such as the national newspapers' move to the "non-union" London Docklands.

Since British shop stewards are actively engaged in collective bargaining, there exists no such separate activity as "worker participation." Collective bargaining is not only concerned with more general labor conditions but also with working conditions at the workplace, which on the continent would be subject to works council competence. The fact that shop stewards combine collective bargaining and worker participation, without distinction between the two activities, has given rise to demands to compensate changes in work organization through more pay. In contrast to the continent, in Great Britain new technologies, or even any management initiative in work organization, are not considered as guaranteed sources of higher productivity, or as sources of higher income in the near future. They are regarded as an infringement on the traditional division of labor between skilled and unskilled, to be compensated in the sphere of labor conditions by more pay. That attitude has given rise to resistance against changes in work organization where wage compensation failed or where the existing division of labor and traditional skills are too undermined. Union opposition to new technology has encouraged unilateral management decision making ("non-union firms") not only for conditions at the workplace but also for general labor conditions (Pontusson 1992).

UNION REPRESENTATION AND WORKS COUNCILS IN GERMANIC EUROPE

The Belgian, Danish and Swedish unions possess extended networks of union representatives or delegates in most industries and even in relatively small enterprises. This is one of the reasons for the high unionization rate in those countries, in addition to the union involvement in social security payments. The networks were established before World War II and have been expanded since. Union representatives are active in social matters, and in large enterprises the chief delegate meets regularly--up to once a week--with management to discuss social problems. The union delegates also constitute the core of the works councils. The parity of works council composition in Belgium and Denmark and the disappearance of the councils in Sweden are a result of the strong union presence within the enterprise, the high unionization rate and the high degree of employer acceptance of union activities within the company. A council consisting solely of employees would be a duplicate of the trade union delegation. Therefore, the council's primary function is not so much to represent the workforce (which is the function of the union delegate), as to serve as a forum where the union delegate, the labor force representative, meets with the employer. The council is not really necessary for this employer-labor force contact, however. In both Belgium and Denmark it is not uncommon for the union delegates to meet with the employer, stop for a short break and then meet again, this time as the official works council, laying down in the minutes what had been discussed before the break. (Neither is it unusual to cancel the second part altogether). Hence, the works council is actually a joint council consisting of the employer and the trade union representation. This function is reinforced by the fact that the higher echelon staff, who are represented on the employer side, do not always occupy their seats. They leave the council work to one or two managers, who chair the meetings.

The German (as well as Austrian and Dutch) "dual system," in which trade unions take care of sector bargaining and autonomous works councils of worker participation, suits a lower rate of organization, a weaker union presence within the firm and more employer opposition to union activities within the company (Thelen 1992). Since the union representation is not able to uphold a claim of representing all enterprise workers, the councils have to perform that function, thereby primarily becoming a representative institution.

Despite the differences in the kind of representative institution--either union representation, works council or both--the nature of worker participation displays great similarities in the Germanic model. Three characteristics stand out. First, there exists some form of integration within managerial decision making. Council members and trade union delegates are usually informed about social developments within the enterprise and about new investments and technologies that have an impact on the level of employment and on working conditions. Almost without exception the councils and the delegates accept any form of technological innovation, and they will try actively to monitor its introduction and more generally the implementation of changes in working conditions.

However, many councils and union delegates complain about the late timing of this information and in practice they are more involved in the phase of implementing change than in the planning and preparatory stages. The influence of works councils and union delegates varies most of all with the subjects at stake and with company size. They exercise more influence in working conditions than in personnel affairs and little influence in economic and financial questions. An exception are economic decisions that have a large and negative impact on the employment level. In those cases not only the worker participation institutions but also the unions as such will be involved and will reinforce the councils' position. In smaller enterprises the employer occupies too dominant a position and exercises too much social control to allow for much influence by the councils or union delegates. In general, however, their influence is greater than in the British or Latin model, according to comparative surveys. Sweden probably occupies a leading position of influence, followed by Germany (Cressey and Williams 1990; Gill and Krieger 1992).

The second characteristic of worker participation in the Germanic model is that the relationship between management and the works council or union representation is rarely one of sustained cold war or overt conflict. Cooperation prevails, not in the sense of easy works council compliance with management proposals but through open discussion, albeit between unequal partners. The obligation to cooperate and to look for common solutions to problems is laid down in the basic agreements or the law. The German law speaks of cooperation based upon mutual trust (*vertrauensvolle Zusammenarbeit*) and explicitly forbids the works council to call strikes.

However, it is less the law that counts than the union and employer associations' role in preventing conflicts. This constitutes the third feature. In case of sustained non-cooperation or latent conflict the unions and sometimes also the employers' organizations use their power to encourage mutual steps in the direction of cooperation and integration. In case of an open breach the organizations assume responsibility for the solution of the conflict. Germany has joint settlement boards (*Einigungsstelle*), but in the sporadic cases in which such a committee is established, the union representatives and management reach an agreement before the neutral chairman has to cast a vote. The three features of integration, cooperation and union coordination--or even discipline--amount to a form of "disciplined integration" of the works council and union representation in managerial decision making (Turner 1991).

Hence, the overall nature of worker participation in Germanic Europe is similar, without much difference between "dual" systems and a union monopoly of worker participation. Simply stated, worker participation works well without works councils. A trade union delegation may do as well, even where the trade union movement is divided, as in Belgium. Crucial to the functioning of worker participation is not institutionalized councils but the separation between labor conditions like wages and working time, handled at industry level, and working conditions and work organization, taken up by worker participation institutions with union supervision and coordination. Collective bargaining at the sector and national levels neutralizes or pacifies the enterprise. This implies that the unions accept management's right to manage, a major union argument to promote sector bargaining. This "employer prerogative" to direct and supervise work has been formulated most explicitly in Scandinavia, where it was stated in the Basic Agreements as well as in sector agreements. In Sweden the employer prerogative, known as "Par. 32" of the Employers' Confederation statutes, was not lifted until the 1976 Worker Participation Act. In other Germanic countries this prerogative was also recognized by the unions, but more implicitly. Worker participation affects the managers' right to manage but does not undermine it. Employees have to be informed about economic and financial decisions but these decisions may be made without worker consent. Social and personnel affairs are subject to the right of consent, but works councils and union representatives are not allowed to wage a conflict.

Like the trade unions themselves, trade union representatives are under a strong obligation to maintain labor peace during the term of a collective agreement. For the unions this amounts to a pledge to prevent autonomous action by the enterprise labor force. By creating a sheltered niche for worker participation, the pacification of the enterprise allows the emergence and the recognition of works councils and union representatives as institutions of cooperation rather than conflict or confrontation.

UNION REPRESENTATION AND WORKS COUNCILS
IN LATIN EUROPE

In Latin Europe cooperative integration is a far less common phenomenon. The relations between works council or union sections and enterprise management are characterized more by mutual confrontation than by cooperation or mutual adaptation. The main obstacle to accommodation does not consist of union efforts to block any managerial initiative that might affect the traditional division of labor, as in Great Britain. Rather, the fact that the enterprise level has remained one of potential conflict over labor conditions prevents cooperative worker participation in the Latin model. Social peace is not enforced to the extent it is in the Germanic model, and neither the unions nor the employers are willing to tie their hands. In practice, many union delegates and works councils accept involvement in social decision. They do not feel any obligation, however, to refrain from more contentious forms of contact with the employer in the course of this involvement or to withdraw in case of spontaneous worker opposition. Although French private sector labor relations are increasingly characterized by union-management accommodation, the unions still do not go further than *cooperation conflictuelle*, a phrase used by one of the socialist trade union confederations. The other side of the coin is the employers' reluctance, or even refusal, to allow for much worker involvement. The Latin management style--the French style in particular--is often referred to as highly authoritarian and hierarchical, with a strong aversion to participation "from below." This rejection of participation has influenced the unions' attitude towards participation and bargaining, but has also been shaped by it. There is a fair chance that participation will lead to union protest and confrontation. To prevent protest, management reduces participation, exemplified by the practice of postponing information to the works council until the time that only the details of implementation are still to be discussed. The lack of a bargaining tradition has left intact the authoritarian character of the French enterprise, and the Latin enterprise in general (Lane 1989).

The difference is confirmed in research published by the European Foundation for the Improvement of Living and Working Conditions in Dublin, a European Union-sponsored institute. Most of the country-specific factors listed in the reports that influence the degree of participation in technology decisions, are actually model-specific, such as management style, union bargaining power, legal regulation and the industrial relations system. This is confirmed by the ranking of the countries. Germanic countries score high, the Latin nations (and Great Britain) score low on each of these points (Gill and Krieger 1992; Gill 1993).

In France, the strained relations have led to the marginalization of the works council, not only by management but also by the unions. Many French works councils concentrate on a few social services--notably the enterprise restaurant (a high priority in France), a library and a number of social events like Christmas parties--rather than on enterprise policies. In Spain, which has one of the highest strike rates in Europe, almost half of the strikes are started by the union delegations (*secciones sindicales*). In both countries unions and employers stay at arms' length and explicitly do not adhere to cooperative integration.

Italy has had a long sequence of worker participation institutions, whose rise and fall reflect more general European trends. They also show the Latin problems of strong inter-union rivalry with efforts of worker mobilization against other unions, spontaneous actions and the unions' need to channel such actions, and the rise of alternative circuits of action and mobilization. In 1943, following more than twenty years of fascism, the confederations concluded a national agreement about the works council, called "internal committee" (*commissione interna*). Such councils had existed before fascism, and had rapidly expanded during the large strike wave in the aftermath of World War I, at the same time as the German councils. To evade the communist-dominated *commissioni*, the mainly Catholic confederation established a rival network of trade union sections. The 1969 Hot Autumn, in which the three union confederations operated in close cooperation, resulted in the rise of two new and spontaneous forms of worker representation-- the *delegati* at the shop floor, and the factory council (*consiglio di fabbrica*), in which all delegates, whether union members or not, acted as a kind of collective trade union representation. The unions tried hard to get these institutions under control. As in most other nations, legislation in Italy was also extended. It introduced a new institution, the "factory union representation," to be elected by the workers, including non-union members. Its main function, however, became one of backing the factory councils, which not only were institutions of worker participation and worker mobilization but also of collective bargaining.

In the early 1980s tension between the Italian confederations increased, fueled by a number of defeats in labor conflicts, including a very large strike at Fiat concerning restructuring and layoffs. The unions then tried a more "cooperative" course. In the public sector a kind of technology agreement, not unlike those elsewhere in Europe, provided for joint consultative committees (*comitati consultativi pariteti*). This new institution was widely imitated throughout Italian industry. However, around 1990 worker committees (*comitati di base* or *cobas*) sprang up in the public sector, as spontaneous forms of worker representation and radical rivals to the unions. In 1993 a national agreement again introduced a new kind of union-dominated works council in private sector companies with at least fifteen employees. Two-thirds of the members are elected by the labor force, the others nominated by the unions.

CO-DETERMINATION

Most European nations have a two-tier management structure for large enterprises. In the most common type a single "managing director" exercises the managerial functions. He is monitored by the second tier, the "management board" or "board of directors." In the second type--prevalent in Germany, Austria and Holland--the management board is the first (and managerial) tier, supervised by a "supervisory board." In both types the second tier has to approve all major investments, mergers, expansions and plant closures. It fires and appoints the managing director (and in the second system also other members of the management board) and coopts its own members. It is comprised mainly of outsiders, including managers from other large companies, bankers, labor law experts and economic experts. France has a different version of the first system, since the managing director also acts as the chairman of the second tier and by doing so exercises almost complete control.

One of the major issues in worker participation has been worker representation on the second tier--the management board or the supervisory board. That form of worker participation is called co-determination (*Mitbestimmung* in Germany), although the terms co-determination and *Mitbestimmung* are also used in a wider sense, to denote all forms of worker participation, including the works councils and trade union representation. The main example of co-determination has been the composition of the supervisory board (*Aufsichtsrat*) in the larger German enterprises. After World War II the trade unions demanded nationalization and *Mitbestimmung*, but the Allied Powers and the Cold War reduced the actual extent of *Mitbestimmung* that was introduced. Since its introduction it has remained a hot issue between unions and employers. More than once the latter have appealed to the Constitutional Court to have the law changed. In practice, German employers have become used to the system. Since 1976 three variations have existed in Germany:

- One-half of the supervisory board seats in large steel works and coal mines. This *Montanmitbestimmung* (*Montan* means mining) approaches most closely the original union demands. In the thirty companies in this group the board is a joint labor force-shareholder council.
- One-half of the supervisory board seats, but with a casting vote for the board president, who is elected by the shareholders. This type of *Mitbestimmung* applies to all companies with over 2,000 workers, some 500 companies.
- One-third of the supervisory board seats in companies with 500 to 2,000 employees; called "one-third parity."

The labor force representatives are works council members. In the first two forms of *Mitbestimmung* union officials may also be elected to the board. The IG Metall chairman himself has long been a member of the board at Mercedes Benz. In those companies the unions also have some influence over the appointment of one member of the management council, the personnel (or personnel and organization) manager (*Arbeitsdirektor*). However, that person is usually a union-friendly labor law or personnel expert, seldom a (former) union official.

Although the board members tend to stress their independence towards any outside institution, the accumulation of worker participation arrangements provides the works councils, and in the larger enterprises also the unions, with early information on important decisions at hand. The timing of the information often determines the degree of influence the councils are able to exercise, since it allows the council or the unions to draw alternative blueprints for reorganization and other changes. Moreover, the procedure for appointing the personnel manager gives the unions influence in the personnel department and provides them with an easy opportunity to recruit new union members among recently hired employees. This has helped to maintain a very high union density among the manual workers in these companies.

Worker representation in the second tier also exists in a few other countries, mainly in the Germanic model. Until the 1960s most unions rejected it because of the responsibility it would entail for enterprise affairs. It became a popular topic in the early 1970s, when the wave of militancy forwarded the search for more "economic democracy." During that period, some trade unions changed their opinion and became advocates of the system, an expression of greater union interest in the enterprise level. Worker representation on the board also exists in France, but in that country the position of the worker representative is weaker, and it hardly adds to the works councils' influence because of the powerful position of the managing director and the prevailing management-union antagonism.

7

From Sector Uniformity to Enterprise Diversity

Under Fordism, most unions were mainly interested in the positive effects of productivity growth and industrial restructuring on the wage level. The combination of productivity and employment as union priorities has been most pronounced in Sweden, where it dates back to the 1950s and has been at the heart of the "Swedish model." Recent changes in economic structure and the rise of unemployment in a number of countries have forced unions to focus on employment effects. Since the oil crises, unions and works councils have actively sought to influence company decisions on enterprise restructuring, in particular aiming at training facilities, employment guarantees and early retirement provisions for older workers. In combination with this change in focus, international attention has shifted from Sweden to Germany, with its works council and union involvement in training programs.

THE SWEDISH MODEL: THE EXAMPLE OF THE 1960s AND 1970s

In the 1960s and 1970s Swedish labor relations were widely acclaimed as an example for the rest of Europe. A high organization rate on both sides allowed employer and union confederations to negotiate national wage agreements. The result was a combination of uniformity and greater equality, in particular between categories of manual workers in various industrial sectors. The unions' "solidaristic wage policy" aimed at a reduction of sector wage differentials by raising wages to the level attained by the more productive sectors. Sectors and enterprises that lagged behind in productivity were forced to restructure or were even forced out of business. Unemployment was stabilized to less than two percent by a very active labor market policy, a common union-employer accomplishment. The main ingredient of this labor market policy consisted of retraining and worker mobility. Unemployed workers were pressed to retrain for new employment in more productive sectors and companies. The result was a continuous process of industrial restructuring and worker mobility, reinforcing Sweden's position as the leading small industrial nation (Delsen 1995).

The recognition of the employer prerogative by the unions encouraged the introduction of new technologies, even more than in the other Germanic countries. Employers had a relatively free hand to improve productivity, and they were pressed to do so by high wage claims. A second feature of the "Swedish model," as it was called, consisted of the social democrats' domination of politics. They expanded social services to all kinds of social policy, reducing the effects of the high labor mobility. Moreover, the social democratic governments, especially in the 1970s, were willing to introduce labor legislation in instances where employers refused to agree with trade unions on major reforms. The social democratic domination of politics has even been regarded as a "countervailing power" to the employer prerogative in the economy. While the employers enjoy a relatively large degree of freedom in the economy, the social effects of their decisions are offset in the political sphere.

This "welfare capitalism," a combination of a capitalist economy and extensive social democratic policies, seemed to function almost as a *perpetuum mobile*, maintaining its smooth movement forward most of the time. However, already in the 1970s a few cracks became visible, and in the 1990s the cracks have dominated any contemporary examination of the Swedish model. The first problem that caused union-employer tension was the extension of worker participation in the 1970s. In response to worker complaints that frequent labor mobility negatively affected worker motivation and social life, the unions demanded more worker participation, but the employers opposed this attack upon their prerogative. The unions then turned to politics, This resulted in the 1976 *Medbestämmandelagen*, admired by unions in the rest of Europe. It obliged employers to negotiate with the trade union any important change within the enterprise that affected labor conditions or employment. Though the law has been used mainly to negotiate redundancies, it strained union-employer relations since it was a greater and a more abrupt change than the changes in the other Germanic nations at that time.

A Swedish union invention, the wage earner funds, formed a second (and more contentious) source of friction. The high wage demands drove some enterprises out of business but still left ample margins for increased pay in the highly productive firms. In order to skim off the resulting surplus profit in these companies, the unions proposed the establishment of wage earner funds. Employers would have to transmit part of this surplus profit into the funds, which would serve as collective investment funds, administered in part by the unions. By making the workers (by means of the unions) collective shareholders, the funds would bring about more equality in economic power and income with individual shareholders. This Meidner Proposal, named after the responsible union economist, became a hotly contested issue in Swedish politics in the 1970s, and the funds were not enacted until 1983, in a weaker version. Five regional funds were set up, in which the unions made up the majority of the board. To prevent a takeover of companies, investment in company shares was set a maximum of ten percent for each company.

The establishment of the funds seriously strained employer-union contacts. The shift to a conservative government during 1976 to 1982 and the large 1980 labor conflict involving clerical workers and the public sector caused additional cracks in the model. Moreover, tensions have arisen between the social democratic confederation and the clerical workers' confederation and also within the social democratic trade union confederation--between the metalworkers union, which is compelled to moderate its wage claims, and unions that profit from wage equality. The rise of public sector and clerical workers' union "cartels" has also reduced the confederations' power over the member unions. The employers increasingly favor a decentralization of bargaining, preferably to the company level. At the end of the 1980s they decided not to participate any longer in the corporatist talks and institutions. Since that time wage bargaining has shifted from the national to the sector level and back, and corporatism is in decline. Moreover, conservative governments partly dismantled the wage earner funds in the late 1980s.

Although the *Medbestämmandelagen* and the Meidner funds have been important and unrivaled social democratic accomplishments, the Swedish centralization no longer seems a viable method for new reforms. The discussion on decentralization throughout Europe makes it even less of a model for the rest of the continent. It has lost its spell, and attention has shifted to Germany.

THE GERMAN MODEL: THE EXAMPLE OF THE 1980s and 1990s

The preceding chapter stressed the distinction between sector-level union-employer bargaining on labor conditions and enterprise-level worker participation in working conditions. However, worker participation may also extend to a form of bargaining between management and works councils or trade union representatives. This kind of bargaining over working conditions, and company personnel and social policies in general, has been studied in particular in the German car industry, where worker participation is exercised by the works councils, in combination with the worker and union representatives in the *Aufsichtsrat.*

Worker participation in Germany is focused most of all on the level of employment, its primary concern being layoffs. That interest is shared by most worker participation institutions throughout Europe. What sets German industry, and in particular the larger car manufacturing companies, apart is that unions and workers not only oppose layoffs but also stress labor mobility within the firm. They would not like superfluous labor to affect company productivity and be the cause of future redundancies.

The combination of high productivity and employment guarantees forces management to look for more advanced production methods and new industrial activities. They can only do so by continuously retraining and providing mobility within the enterprise for workers who would otherwise have been laid off. The works councils and the unions are actively involved in the process of enterprise-related retraining in a variety of skills, as well as job mobility within the company, as major preconditions of high productivity combined with employment guarantees. Technological innovation, manpower planning, vocational training and worker mobility within the enterprise are subjects of regular bargaining between "productivity coalitions" consisting of the worker participation institutions and the company management.

In particular Streeck has contributed to the focus on training in the international labor relations literature. Streeck emphasizes the positive side of this bargaining relationship within the enterprise. It puts serious constraints upon management by ruling out layoffs, but by doing so it forces management to look for new productive potentials within the enterprise and to seek diversified high-quality production. The works councils support this strategy by promoting broad training activities and internal worker mobility. This kind of employment security stimulates an internal labor market within the enterprise. A negative social effect is that it fences off the company from outside job-seekers (Streeck 1984, 1992).

A comparison of the Swedish solidaristic wage policy and the German "productivity coalitions" between works councils, unions and management with policies in other countries reveals a number of similarities. The positive attitude towards technological change is shared by all unions in the Germanic countries. Unions embrace technological change as the major vehicle for maintaining national or sector competitive power. A prominent example was the 1954 Joint Declaration on Productivity, signed by the Belgian union and employer confederations, in which they pledged their mutual support for technological change. The Swedish and the German union concern with employment also exists in the rest of the continent. It is expressed in demands for employment policies, union involvement in labor market policies, union acceptance of labor mobility and their involvement in training activities, or their support of such activities by employers and the state.

This union policy differs from that in Great Britain, where unions compete for employment. Craft unions try to defend their traditional skilled workers' job control and job security, if necessary, against the introduction of new technologies and the employment of other categories of workers. The craft unions' main priority is job security, the guarantee to retain one's own job, not employment security, implying the acceptance of mobility and retraining. In the British case, sectional interests prevail over the wider interest of technological progress and national competitive power.

In Latin Europe the union focus is more general. Technological change is accepted as a base of higher future wages, but it is also considered an employer weapon to fight the unions, and, first of all, to dismiss union activists. The latter attitude may prevail at times, or even most of the time, motivating the unions to fight changes in technology and work organization. The technology agreements of the early 1980s, providing for more information in all phases of planning, preparation, introduction and implementation of technological change, have not reduced these differences in basic attitudes between the three models of labor relations.

The Swedish and the German developments also show major differences with each other and with the other Germanic countries. The Swedish position stands out because of its direct stimulation of national labor mobility and retraining, as parts of a national labor market policy. In other countries the unions have shown a more passive attitude towards new technology, waiting for its introduction and trying to mitigate its labor market effects by making employment a union demand in national or sector bargaining. The unions in the Low Countries have sometimes given up wage claims for employment guarantees, not only in enterprises but also for each sector. They lack the strong involvement of the Swedish and German unions in training and other labor market measures, however.

Three points seem to add to the relevance of the German experience when compared to that of Sweden, in addition to the fact that the strong social democratic position in Sweden is an exceptional one in Europe. First, the German unions have stressed training activities even more than their Swedish counterparts. The Swedish unions' first priority has actually been with redistribution, as the core of their solidaristic wage policy. Other goals, like labor market mobility and training activities, have been second to this aim of increased equality. The German works councils, supported by the unions, regard employment as their main concern, but productivity growth is closely linked with it and is even more of a daily concern than employment.

Second, and more important, is that the Swedish union interest in productivity and training focuses on the nation and the sector, while the German works councils are also concerned with enterprise productivity. Since company continuity rather than sector survival has always been the overriding employer concern, the German union interest is closer to the employers' heart. It does allow for real productivity coalitions between works councils and employers, sharing responsibility for the future of the individual company. Streeck speaks of the German productivity coalitions as a system of "enterprise corporatism," in contrast to the pluralist competition of British unions within the enterprise. Indeed, the German system shares some of the main features of corporatism, such as a monopoly of interest aggregation by the works councils, enforcement of the bargaining results, influence on the company's social and economic policy, and a foundation based on a kind of social partnership. But it does not exclude others from participating in the works council elections. (Turner 1991; Thelen 1992).

Third, in Sweden manual and clerical workers are addressed by separate trade union confederations, while the German unions organize both categories of workers. This difference affects sector and national bargaining most of all. It also has an impact on enterprise labor relations since it allows the German works councils to speak more authoritatively on behalf of the whole enterprise labor force (Thelen 1993).

The differences between Sweden and Germany concern the locus of power and the focus of interests. The Swedish unions show what strong organization and centralization are capable of. The German unions show a combination of enterprise-level strength, embodied in the works councils, and sector force. Union centralization at sector level supports and reinforces the works councils' position, and it may compensate for the works councils' weaknesses. A balance of power between the sector and the enterprise gives the unions the possibility to shift resources from one level to another, albeit within the limits set by the works council quest for autonomy.

THE RISE OF THE LOCAL UNION

Since the 1980s new production concepts have flooded Europe, originating in the United States and, even more so, in Japan. The latter country has conquered a sizable part of the European automobile and electronics market and its production methods and labor relations have become popular research items and discussion topics in Europe. In general, the new concepts point to a shift from uniform mass production of highly standardized products to a more diversified and specialized production tailored to specific demands--a shift from "Fordism" to what provisionally has been labeled "Post-Fordism." The mass market, served by large stocks of identical products, is giving way to a myriad of small niche markets, which require quick changes in the production process. Terms like "lean production" and "just-in-time-production" refer to the shift in emphasis from quantity to quality, from uniformity to flexibility.

These changes are affecting the structure of private enterprise. During the time of mass production, large companies often contained all stages of the production process. This "vertical" structure is being replaced by a "horizontal" structure, consisting of subsidiaries which control a significant part of the production process. Relatively small and rather autonomous subsidiaries, or product groups, are substituting for large and hierarchically organized company divisions, and parts of the production process are distributed to external suppliers. The latter may be formally independent, but in fact their functioning is completely determined by the needs of the larger companies. Flexible adjustment of the larger companies to market conditions requires flexible adaptation of the subcontracting enterprises to the larger firms. The main firms' need for flexibility not only determines the subcontractors' production schedules, but indirectly their working conditions as well. The difference between company subsidiaries and external subcontractors may in fact be a small one, since the subsidiaries also have to compete with external subcontractors when marketing their products within the company they belong to.

The changes in production processes, economic structure and production schedules have had two major effects on labor relations: A partial decentralization of collective bargaining from the sector to the enterprise and the introduction of new forms of worker participation. The former affects the bargaining level, the latter the existing forms and structures of worker participation, with the overall effect of bringing the two activities closer to one another.

The changes, in combination with the developments in labor force and union membership discussed in Chapter 4, have recently drawn more attention to the union representation within the enterprise and the local union. The point was stressed by Locke in a survey of Italian industrial restructuring and variations in union involvement in it. While the unions failed to exercise any influence at the Fiat automobile works, they were successfully involved in the restructuring of the Alfa Romeo car plant and the textile industry in northern Italy. Locke points not so much to union participation in training but to a number of local conditions, like local traditions of union-employer cooperation and union militancy and links between the unions and local politics, which provide the unions with power resources within the enterprise. More characteristic is that success is always reached without any support by the sector unions or the union confederation. The latter are paralyzed by mutual conflict and union-state conflicts. The local unions successfully overcome the ideological split between the confederations and they operate in close cooperation, made possible by the fact that the employment issue hardly gives rise to any ideological controversy. It is not the locals' dependence upon the unions but their autonomy from higher union levels that makes for success (Locke 1990, 1992; Hancké 1993). This probably specifically applies to the Latin countries, with their greater degree of tension and rivalry between the national union confederations. Most authors agree, however, that in general the close interaction between strong trade unions at the sector level and the local union involved in enterprise decisions is the best guarantee of union success. Germany is often cited as the example of this two-level union strategy, but it exists in the other Germanic nations as well.

THE DECENTRALIZATION OF COLLECTIVE BARGAINING

In industry, as well as in services--which have been subject to similar processes of automation--the shift to flexible supply has increased the need for worker flexibility and mobility within the firm. It has given rise to flexi-time-- labor contracts which no longer provide for a full-time work week but for various forms of part-time work, including total flexibility ranging from zero to forty hours a week, depending on the availability of work. Women in particular are employed in part-time jobs, and in some countries, particularly in Holland, the growth of female employment has almost completely been confined to part-time work. The unions resist the trend to part-time work as a threat to normal full-time employment. However, the expansion of part-time work has to some extent also been a response to demand, especially by women (Delsen 1995).

To do justice to the flexibility in working and labor conditions, and deriving strength from the economic conditions, employers are increasingly promoting a decentralization of wage bargaining from the sector to the enterprise and even from the enterprise to the plant (Katz 1993). This decentralization is the second effect of industrial restructuring, but it has also been influenced by economic conditions, in particular the high unemployment level of the 1980s and the 1990s in most European countries. Employers expect that data on unemployment impress workers more when related to the company's economic position instead of the sector as a whole. Some employers even propagate bargaining with the works councils rather than with the unions. The trend towards enterprise bargaining has figured highly in all discussion on collective bargaining since the early 1980s (Mueller and Purcell 1992). Indeed, it seems to be a major current trend in European labor relations, despite the fact that even employers have sometimes favored a stabilization of or return to bargaining at sector level, to counter the strong bargaining position of the unions in high-productivity firms. Great Britain has probably been affected most. Whatever tradition there was of multi-employer bargaining rather than sector bargaining has disappeared again, due to the trend of more flexibility and to the anti-union labor legislation of the 1980s (Grahl and Teague 1989). At the same time the anti-union legislation of the Conservative governments has undermined the power base of the shop stewards as negotiators, for instance by attacking the closed shop. One of the laws secured "employment protection" for workers who refuse to become union members or cancel their union membership, by declaring illegal any employer sanctions against such non-compliant workers.

In the Germanic model, decentralization means more room for enterprise-level decision making within the framework of less elaborate sector agreements, rather than a real shift from sector to enterprise bargaining. Company provisions especially cover new arrangements in working time--not only flexi-time and part-time labor contracts but also the elaboration of the full-time work week. Reduction of the work week has become one of the main union strategies to reduce unemployment. IG Metall leads the way with its demand for a 35-hour work week and unions in the other countries are following the example. The reduction in work hours is opposed by most employers, who complain about the negative impact on production schedules and who promote more flexibility instead.

However, the general labor conditions are still laid down in sector agreements, and while most employers may advocate a more complete decentralization, they are reluctant to take the first step by themselves (Bercusson 1993). In Scandinavia decentralization has meant to some extent a shift from the national to the sector level, rather than to the enterprise. In Austria and Germany the position of sector bargaining stands as yet unchallenged, although the sector agreements leave more room for elaboration by the works councils. In the Low Countries the number of enterprise agreements is growing steadily, but the great majority of workers is still covered by sector agreements and enterprise bargaining remains coordinated by the sector unions and the national confederations.

In the Latin model the shift towards enterprise bargaining is more widespread. Bargaining has been affected by two features of the prevailing model of labor relations: regular government efforts to stimulate collective bargaining and the influence of the relatively large public sector. A prominent example of government stimulation consists of the legislation initiated by Jean Auroux, French minister of Labor, in the early 1980s. The main thrust of the "Auroux Laws" has been to encourage enterprise collective bargaining. The laws oblige employers to negotiate wages and working time regularly with the trade union sections. Despite initial employer resistance, the obligation has resulted in a large number of formal enterprise agreements. The extension of company bargaining and the formalization at that level because of the legal provisions hide various forms of decision making, however. Many employers prefer to deal with the *comité d'entreprise*, which has a longer tradition of cooperation than the union representatives, is more ready to comply with employer proposals and contains a growing share of non-union members. Rather than the unions enforcing the obligation to bargain upon the employers, the procedure has been the reverse, with the employers enforcing it upon the works council. This may amount to complete unilateral decision making by the employer, and it contributes to the further decline of trade union influence.

In general the public sector has given the example of enterprise rather than sector bargaining, and in a more cooperative way than in the private sector. Following this example, collective bargaining in the private sector is also shifting to the company level in Latin Europe, and it is increasingly characterized by some form of employer-union cooperation. Its main topics are the same as in Germanic Europe, including working time flexibility and employment guarantees in case of enterprise restructuring. Although some see new horizons of collective bargaining Germanic style, Latin bargaining is plagued by the weak position--in France even the virtual absence--of the union sections and by the regular shift to the political arena. On the Iberian Peninsula union efforts to engage in enterprise bargaining are motivated by the disappointing results of tripartism rather than by a positive shift in union focus. The role of the public sector as a pioneer in Latin labor relations is currently decreasing. It has always been limited in Spain, and has been affected by privatization programs in France and Portugal. Despite the extent of the French public sector strikes in December 1995, their isolation also showed the reduced role of that sector. In former times such strikes would certainly have been imitated in the private sector.

In sum, there is a general European trend towards decentralization, but it is limited in the Germanic model and not highly motivated at either side in the Latin model despite the formalization of bargaining in the latter.

EMPLOYEE PARTICIPATION IN THE 1990s

Worker participation has also been affected by a series of new developments and innovations. One important development is the spread of teamwork, in which small groups share responsibility for their output and sometimes even for the total production process of one or more products. Work teams had already been introduced in the 1970s, at the time of economic democracy and the struggle against worker alienation, but they gained momentum when Japanese "quality circles" were brought to Europe in the late 1970s and early 1980s. The introduction of work teams has various roots. Their rise in the 1970s was mainly stimulated by social scientists, who advocated the need for a more diversified working life as a contribution to the quality of life. It was a reaction to the degrading effects of mass production, in which workers were repeating the same few activities every few minutes.

The quality circles and related changes, sometimes extending to worker involvement in total "quality management," are mainly a management initiative, introduced to motivate workers and to increase productivity and product quality. This Japanese invention also pays some attention, however, to the quality of working life. Quality circles have probably become most widespread in France as a management device to reduce the role of the union representatives, but they have been introduced in other nations as well, and they are operative in more than half of the larger German firms. In general quality circles do not threaten or supplant the existing channels of worker participation. In Germanic Europe they are often set up in close management-works council cooperation. However, the management-initiated forms of increased worker responsibility have created problems for the trade unions. Trade unions, to some extent stressing divergent rather than common interests between employee and employer, are increasingly considered as outside intruders, spoiling the relationship between employee and company. The new worker responsibilities intensify the relationship between worker and enterprise and encourage the integration of the worker within the company. This integration, reinforced by enterprise-provided fringe benefits and social and recreational facilities, has become known as the Japanization of labor relations. It focuses on the interests the employer and the employees have in common, minimizing their differences in interests and the need for independent trade unions.

On the other hand, the unions do not oppose improvements in working conditions and in worker participation. To solve this dilemma, a number of unions have proposed their own version of more worker involvement and influence in working conditions, like IG Metall's ideas of teamwork (*Gruppenarbeit*), as part of a campaign to humanize labor (*Humanisierung der Arbeit*). The initiatives do not conflict with management-promoted forms of worker participation, but the unions stress the right to elect the group leaders, demand time for group discussion and seek higher pay to compensate for more responsibility. These three versions of group activity and shared responsibility are combined in new management strategies like Human Resources Management (HRM), which no longer regards workers as a collective cost to be reduced, but recognizes each worker as a valuable asset to be invested in. A new direction in labor psychology and organizational sciences, "socio-technics" tries to combine the new approaches towards workers with changes in company design. In accordance with this change from "worker" to "employee" and of industrial relations to "employee-relations," employers also advocate the individualization of labor and working conditions, including individual pay schemes. The transition from sector or company productivity to individual employee productivity as the major parameter for wage increases is strongly opposed by the unions. They argue that it might well lead to renewed worker dependence on managerial decision making in labor conditions, and that it undermines union wage solidarity efforts.

In France, the Auroux reforms have not only stimulated collective bargaining but also introduced changes in worker participation. They widened the competency of the works councils and the trade union delegates. This part of the legislation did not produce the intended effect, however. Union implantantion within French enterprise and union influence have remained weak. A more innovative reform consists of the *groupes d'expression.* They allow workers to express their views in a form of direct democracy, without any union or works council intermediation, as part of a new kind of worker "citizenship." The idea is in line with the traditional French idea of spontaneous worker initiative and enterprise democracy, advocated most of all by the socialist union, which had supported such ideas since 1968. The unions have signed thousands of enterprise agreements providing for *groupes d'expression*, despite fear of some erosion of their own role within the enterprise. The overall impact of the new institution has been limited, however. The number of workers covered remains rather small, and the groups have not been able to overcome employer resistance to their independence. Many of the groups have actually functioned as quality circles, or their meetings have become a mere ritual. The local union is a weak institution in France, but direct democracy without the unions in the form of the "expression groups" has even less influence (Regini 1993).

The French developments are an extreme expression of the wider European trend. Formal rules have extended the scope of worker participation, but the economic conditions, changes in the composition of the work force and the decline in union density have provided employers the opportunity to introduce their own participation devices or to use the formal institutions to their own advantage.

8

Labor Conditions in Europe

In most of Europe, labor conditions have been the subject of collective bargaining and of legislation. The latter has been of particular importance in the field of health and safety and in social security. While health and safety regulations are still being extended, social security has fallen victim to government attempts to implement cuts in spending. Moreover, there has been a shift in attention from social security to employment policies as a core feature of the European "welfare state."

WAGES

Union involvement in wage bargaining has been guided by three central goals: wage predictability, wage increase and wage equality. Only the first one, wage predictability, is generally shared by employers. The desire for wage predictability has been expressed in the struggle to fix occupational or industry wage rates for one or two years and at time rather than piece rates. The early fixed-wage rates were originally aimed at preventing arbitrary employer decisions on wages and "unfair" wage competition by low-pay firms. Once some form of uniformity in wage rates was reached, the unions focused on wage adaptation to rising prices, a major issue in twentieth century collective bargaining and conflict. As a principle, wage adjustments for inflation have generally been accepted, but the way in which it is done has remained a source of conflict between unions and employers, and sometimes with the national government. Among trade unions the most popular form of wage predictability has been wage indexation, consisting of automatic wage increases with rising prices. This automatic adaptation has existed in Belgium since the 1920s (*index*), and in Italy since the end of World War II (*scala mobile*). In countries where wages are not adapted automatically, most collective agreements provide for a wage increase which at least covers the current rate of inflation. Sometimes they include an extra rise if the inflation increases (Flanagan, Soskice, and Ulman 1983).

Automatic wage adaptation has a few disadvantages for the unions. It reduces the room for further bargaining and easily gives workers the impression that the adaptation is not a union accomplishment. Unions feel that at a five percent inflation rate a seven percent wage increase looks more impressive than two percent plus inflation. The British unions have been most sensitive on this point, probably related to the greater degree of competition among the unions and the importance of informal bargaining. In other countries national governments tend to oppose automatic adaptation because it fuels inflation, an attitude that has been reinforced since the oil crises.

Union efforts to secure wage increases along with adjustments for inflation have been expressed in the link between productivity growth and wage increases. Since the 1960s the combination of price rise and productivity growth has been accepted on the continent as the major parameter of wage increase in any new agreement, even though part of the amount may actually be used for working time reduction or other improvements in labor conditions. Even British "productivity agreements" in the 1960s based increases on this link. Due to the economic conditions since the early 1980s recent agreements have often contained lower wage increases than the rise in productivity. In particular large companies in trouble have tried to reduce wage increases or even introduce wage decreases for one or more years, sometimes in combination with employment guarantees. Indeed, in the last decade employment has been the guiding principle in wage formation and has prompted the unions to engage in "concession bargaining," in which unions give up some well-established wage principles or accept incidental wage reductions as concessions for employment guarantees. As a general principle, however, the formula "wage increase equals price rise plus (sector) productivity growth" still stands in most of Europe. Any deviation is subject to hot debate and is only accepted as a means to safeguard employment (Flanagan, Soskice, and Ulman 1983).

Wage equality has been of more concern to the industrial unions, which organize skilled as well as unskilled workers, than to the British craft unions. Equality was one of the arguments used in the 1960s to centralize wage bargaining in a number of countries, since it would allow wage increases to be linked to national rather than sector productivity growth. A second way to arrive at greater wage equality has been to express wage demands in absolute amounts rather than in percentages. This is not common, however, due to opposition by skilled and clerical workers.

The strongest measure to increase low wages has been the introduction of a minimum wage. This device varies along the lines of the labor relations models. In Great Britain and Ireland neither a statutory minimum wage nor sector minimum rates apply. Wage rates in unorganized and "sweating" branches in Britain, like the retail trade and hotel and catering services, used to be set by joint employer-union Wage Councils. In 1994, however, the councils fell victim to the Conservative drive for deregulation and anti-union measures. In most Germanic countries either a national statutory minimum wage or sector minimum rates have been in force since World War II. Both of them are actually determined by employer-union bargaining, since the statutory minimum wage often follows trends in collective bargaining. In France and on the Iberian Peninsula legal minimum wages are in effect. The French "growth-related" statutory minimum wage, *salaire minimum interprofessionel de croissance* SMIC, has more impact on collective bargaining than the minimum wage in Germanic countries, since a sizable minority of French sectors still have wage scales which contain pay levels below the minimum--in which case workers are paid the SMIC. In most other nations the number of people directly affected by the minimum wage is below five or six percent, but the legal minimum wage often also functions as a parameter for increases in social security benefits. Young workers up to the age of twenty-one or twenty-three are entitled to a percentage of the minimum, related to their age.

The minimum wage has not affected the wage gap between manual and clerical workers. Traditionally, clerical workers have enjoyed privileges in all kinds of labor conditions, including more extensive legal protection of their labor conditions than manual workers. Until the 1970s this disparity was generally accepted as the norm, and a strict distinction was made between the two categories. In line with the quest for more equality in living conditions, rather than just in labor conditions, and with the growing "clericalization" of the labor force the differences became a major topic in the 1970s and 1980s, along with greater equality in working time and social security. This "levelling" has contributed to the growth of separate clerical workers' federations since the 1970s, which defend their members' "privileges." The manual-clerical disparity has lost some of its saliency in the 1990s because of the general change towards thinking in terms of differentiation rather than equality and because the national union confederations take care not to alienate clerical workers any further.

Regional wage disparities have been a traditional union concern only in Italy. Sector bargaining in the smaller nations generally leads to national wage uniformity within the sectors. In the larger countries variations in cost of living are sometimes taken into account by means of premiums for workers in the national capital and other cities. Italy has large regional differences between wages in the industrialized North and the less developed South, however. The potential impact of low wage migration from the South to the North has motivated the unions to look for greater equality between the two parts of the country. A recent and unprecedented effort to reduce regional disparities is currently under way in the former communist eastern part of Germany. The German unions are eager to bring the wage level in the new federal states on a par with those in the rest of the nation. This is not merely an expression of their concern with equality. It would also prevent any impact of low wages in the eastern part of the country on the labor market and of collective bargaining in the western part. Employers base their objections against this equality drive on the large differences in productivity, which should be reflected in wage disparities. In 1992 they took the unprecedented step of canceling a wage agreement which provided for full parity by 1994, claiming it was too expensive and would lead to even more unemployment in the East. Since then full wage equality has been postponed for a couple of years.

Gender inequality is a fourth form of inequality addressed by the unions. It is not a traditional union interest, but it reached the bargaining agenda under pressure by the second feminist movement, the growing female participation rate and European Union activity in the field. Despite some progress, full parity has not been reached, and, even more important, women still crowd the lower paid functions and are underrepresented in high-pay functions. More than twice as many women than men "enjoy" the minimum wage in their sector or nation.

While employers have shared the positive union attitude towards wage predictability, they have not been responsive to wage equality, arguing that a drive to increase lower wage rates would have the effect of a general wage increase. Also they fear that it would increase enterprise competition to recruit workers for higher paying jobs. Part of the wage drift in enterprises, in addition to wage rates agreed upon in collective bargaining, can be explained by the better paid workers' efforts to maintain some wage differentials and employer efforts to keep better paid workers. Sweden has probably come closest to full equality because of the unions' long-lasting solidaristic wage policy. Wage inequality between sectors and categories of workers is still very pronounced in Austria, where the trade unions have stressed employment rather than wage equality.

Two forms of extra pay commonly found in some countries are profit sharing and capital sharing. The first consists of a premium at the end of the year financed by the enterprise profits. This has often taken the form of a "thirteenth month" of pay, albeit not always a full month. In France, President De Gaulle promoted this profit sharing in 1959 as a conservative policy of worker integration in the enterprise. In 1967 De Gaulle also introduced legal rules for providing workers with company shares. In the 1980s French governments of various composition extended the legal rules. While profit sharing (*interessement*) applies to less than two million French workers, capital sharing (*participation*) agreements cover almost five million workers, an unrivalled position in Europe (Uvalic 1993). Recently, capital sharing has become popular in other countries as well, due to the clericalization of the labor force and the need to motivate highly trained workers in the enterprise. All capital sharing agreements provide shares for the individual worker. No other country has followed the Swedish example of collective investment funds. While most unions have supported both profit and capital sharing, their attitude has also been guided by the argument that profit sharing especially might affect wage predictability and should not affect "normal" pay rates.

In the mid-1990s two issues are dominating wage bargaining and conflict: the relation between wages and unemployment and the relation between pay and individual performance. One of the more pressing recent concerns is youth unemployment. This problem is attributed in part to the steady rise of the minimum wage, which has increased the threshold costs of employing young and inexperienced workers. In all of Europe employers have advocated lower youth rates in order to alleviate the problem. In France an effort by the conservative government in 1994 to implement such a reduction by introducing unpaid "learning days," met with fierce opposition, demonstrations and street riots. The measure was cancelled. The issue remains on the agenda throughout Europe, however, and trade unions are slowly shifting to more positive attitudes, despite the dangers involved for the rest of the "wage structure," in case the lowest rates are reduced.

Performance-related pay has become an employer favorite, and a major issue in bargaining. Traditionally, part of the industrial labor force has been paid piece rates. Over time union pressure has contributed to its decline and the general spread of time rates. Recently, employers have criticized collective time rates in accordance with their promotion of individual flexibility in working conditions, human resource management and more attention to individual work careers. The new forms of performance-related pay are probably most common in Great Britain, with its lack of industry-wide bargaining. A great majority of the larger British enterprises have adopted premiums, bonuses, merit pay and profit sharing as forms of performance-related wage pay. Wage flexibility has also made headway on the continent, however. A few German firms have even quit their sectoral employers' organizations in order to introduce performance-related pay, rather than follow sector wage scales.

WORKING TIME

The same arguments, employment and flexibility that currently dominate wage bargaining are even more pronounced in the discussion on working time. Since the introduction of the eight-hour workday at the end of World War I, unions have mainly forwarded two arguments for working time reduction: the increase in work load due to new technologies, and the fight against unemployment. Although the former argument is still used, the latter currently predominates, and the main union concern has been to create new jobs. Germany's IG Metall has taken the lead by demanding a general reduction of the work week to thirty-five hours. Other unions and nations have followed, and in most of Europe the forty-hour work week, implemented in the 1970s (to some extent also as a means to fight unemployment), was replaced in the 1980s by thirty-seven or thirty-eight hours and still less for clerical workers. A spectacular move was made in 1993, when IG Metall accepted a proposal to safeguard employment at Volkswagen: a four-day work week in exchange for a twenty percent wage cut. The step has prompted many negative responses by employers and unions alike, but it has been imitated by a few other enterprises. Recent French legislation has provided financial support for firms wishing to reduce the work week. Originally the aim of the law was a reduction to thirty-two hours. This piece of legislation again shows the general difference between the Germanic model, where state measures tend to follow existing practice, and the Latin model, where they try to produce new practice.

Employment considerations have also encouraged the extension of early retirement benefits before the formal retirement age, which stands at sixty to sixty-five years in most of Europe. State-supported schemes have allowed workers in sectors plagued by high unemployment or in companies with mass redundancies to opt for a *pre-pension*, as it is called in French. Sometimes the firms are under formal obligation to fill the vacancies by recruiting young workers. However, from a device to fight youth unemployment (in combination with lower wages for younger workers), early retirement has gradually become an advantage for employees who are still at work. This also applies to the extension of holidays to four or five weeks--often with extra pay for part of that period--originally motivated by employment concerns more than by increasing workload. The long holidays allow many workers to enjoy one-week spring holidays in addition to three- or four-week summer holidays, partly as an expression of solidarity with the unemployed. Other forms of longer leave, like educational leave, have also become popular subjects of discussion, without much practical effect until now. The rising costs of the early retirement provisions have motivated governments and employers to replace it by a flexible retirement age, between 55 and 70, with proportional adaptation of old age benefits. In January 1996, right after the French public sector strikes against government measures to reduce early retirement, the German government introduced a flexible retirement system after long consultations with the national confederations and as part of a wider "pact" to fight rising unemployment.

The need for more enterprise flexibility is expressed in employer demands to spread work over more than five days, including Saturday--a major bone of contention in Germany, where the unions resist this attack on the "weekend off," regarded as one of the major postwar union accomplishments. Recent collective agreements meet employer demands for more flexibility in work hours during the year by stipulating annual rather than weekly working hours, leaving some room for adaptation of working time, within strict limits, to busy and slack periods.

A topic which has gained much attention lately is the rise of atypical work, in the form of part-time and temporary-work contracts. In particular the share of part-time work has increased; in Scandinavia and Holland it applies to over one quarter of the labor force, most of them female workers in half-time jobs. While the spread of part-time jobs is due mainly to the demand for such contracts by employees, the growth of temporary work is less voluntary and mainly results from employer policies. The latter are often reluctant to introduce part-time contracts since they increase labor costs and actually may decrease labor flexibility. The trade unions still reject both part-time and temporary work as potential threats to their predominantly full-time (and male) members. The expansion of part-time work has prompted European Union directives and national legislation in a number of countries, providing or extending dismissal protection and social insurance coverage for the part timers.

While most part-time work at least offers a predictable income, there are other, more "precarious" forms of part-time employment which do not. They include variable working weeks--ranging from total flexibility (from zero to forty hours a week) to other and smaller variations in work hours dependent upon enterprise needs--as well as temporary employment by means of commercial and non-commercial temporary work agencies. This kind of flexibility is expanding, but it still applies to a very small segment of the labor force. In most countries legal rules pertaining to temporary work agencies have been extended recently (Delsen 1995).

FROM HEALTH AND SAFETY TO WORK ENVIRONMENT

Health and safety at work have been old fields of state policies, in particular concerning safety regulations in the coal mines. Early in the nineteenth century national labor offices were set up in a number of countries to check safety conditions and address complaints by individual workers and later also by trade unions. At the end of the nineteenth century worker insurance for industrial accidents became one of the first risks to be covered by social security legislation. The laws shifted responsibility from the worker, who until then had been left without income, to the employer, who was obliged to insure the employees. Downplayed in favor of higher wages in the 1950s and 1960s, the issue of health and safety was featured on the political agenda again in the 1970s. Most current European health and safety laws date from that decade. In the 1980s the European Union became active in the field and issued a number of directives, prompting a revision and extension of existing national legislation.

In a number of countries specific committees exist which concentrate on health and safety issues, such as the French *comité d'hygiène, de sécurité et des conditions de travail*, CHSCT. Like most health and safety committees, the CHSCT is a joint management-worker institution. In other countries the works council addresses these concerns, but it will often have a specific committee for health and safety, or for working conditions more generally, like the Dutch *Arbo* committees. In some countries the enterprise labor force has the right to elect "safety delegates," while in others they are appointed by management in cooperation with the works council. There are no major differences between the three models of labor relations in this field. Even Great Britain and Ireland have laws obliging employers to appoint safety representatives or set up safety committees. In most countries such a legal obligation applies to enterprises of at least ten to twenty employees, a lower threshold than for works councils or other worker representation institutions.

In the 1970s the health and safety issue was widened, addressing not only safety but also the work environment in general. New legislation covered not just industrial injuries, but all forms of physical and mental problems stemming from working conditions. National reports on the number of persons involved and their rate of absence directed even more attention to working conditions in the 1980s. Rules have been tightened and sanctions against non-compliant firms have become stricter. Under the influence of Japanese firms, reducing absenteeism has become a major concern of European companies.

Current issues in the working environment are protection against sexual harassment and overexposure to display screen equipment, and efforts to discourage smoking at the workplace. These three issues have also been addressed by the European Union. The attention to sexual harassment is part of a wider European Union policy on the position of women. Most trade unions have picked up the issue only hesitantly, despite efforts of the women's movement to place the issue on the unions' and the political agenda. Protection from display screen exposure followed after the revolution in information technology and the spread of personal computers. Unions have advocated strict limits on the working time spent at computer screens, but the office working environment is outside their traditional scope and influence. The measures against smoking are part of wider efforts to make smokers aware of the dangers for themselves and for their fellow workers. In many public offices smoking has been banned altogether.

SOCIAL SECURITY AND THE EUROPEAN WELFARE STATE

Many collective agreements in Europe provide for social security benefits, in addition to legal provisions. This kind of social security covers work accidents, illness, unemployment, old age, and childbirth. Where legal provisions exist, the agreements provide for higher benefits or for a longer benefit period, financed by employers and workers alike. Together with taxes the social security contributions make up the difference between net and gross wages, which in some countries surpasses fifty percent of net wages. This disparity between net and gross earnings has become an increasing concern, and governments are looking for ways to reduce this share as one of the means to reduce labor costs.

In combination with state-provided social security these sector-based benefits constitute the core of the European welfare state. In a number of countries one-quarter or more of the national product is spent on them. Because of their importance a short historical note is provided.

Not counting age-old charity, European social security dates back to the early union efforts to cover a few risks, like the friendly societies in nineteenth century Britain. In 1881 the conservative German Chancellor Otto von Bismarck set in motion a trend towards more general coverage. He made work accident and illness insurance obligatory. Work accident insurance was financed by the employers, since that risk was considered inherent to industrial activity; other risks were paid by employers' and workers' contributions. Bismarck's main aim was to stop the rise of socialism and to integrate workers into national society and for that reason his program was confined to manual workers. Other nations followed this example, and at the turn of the century a true wave of social legislation was passed, mostly starting with work accident insurance. Social legislation was stimulated by economic growth and social democratic (and other socialist) publications on bad living conditions. In a number of countries employers and workers paid part of the insurance, as in the Bismarckian scheme; in others the state subsidized trade union insurance funds. The wave of social legislation was interrupted by World War I, but the Russian revolution and the international turmoil during the aftermath of the war stimulated a new and short wave that lasted until unemployment started to rise in 1920. The main outcome of this second wave was not so much social security as the eight-hour workday. The 1930s crisis did not really stimulate new legislation but made the costs of unemployment insurance a hot issue, particularly in Germany where it contributed to the collapse of the Weimar republic (Rimlinger 1971; Flora and Alber 1981).

After 1945 the Bismarckian types of social security--covering manual workers, financed by employer-worker contributions and providing benefits related to previous income--were challenged by a completely new type, advocated by William Beveridge. Beveridgian social security was state-financed and provided low and flat rates for the population as a whole in case of any disability to work, regardless of previous earnings. Additional benefits for those with higher earnings were to be secured on an individual basis, or collectively by means of collective agreements. After this war the social democrats became strong supporters of this Beveridgian system of national social security, while Christian democrats and the political right continued to favor the Bismarckian differentiation between manual and clerical workers and the relation between benefits and previous income (De Swaan 1988). As a consequence, two types of social security emerged. The first was state-provided or subsidized Beveridgian flat rates for the entire population in Great Britain and Scandinavia, where social democrats were in power during the period of postwar reconstruction. The second type consisted of a mixture of pre-war Bismarckian elements for manual workers supplemented with a few Beveridgian elements, in particular in old age pensions, on the rest of the continent, under Christian Democratic or conservative rule (Flora 1986).

In the 1950s a further differentiation took place within the Beveridgian group. While Great Britain stuck to flat rates, to be supplemented by individual effort, Sweden, leading the Scandinavian countries, in 1957 introduced a full contribution-related benefit system in old age pension reform for the population as a whole, without any need for additional individual insurance. This pension reform put an end to the privileged position of clerical workers under either system, who often enjoyed higher benefits or earnings-related benefits.

Since that time a distinction has been commonly made between three groups of welfare states. The first is Scandinavia, with general social security coverage for almost the total population and high benefits. The second is the rest of the continent, with a number of social security programs and manual-clerical differentiation, as well as high benefits. In level of expenditure the Germanic countries score higher than the Latin countries. Great Britain forms the third group, characterized by general coverage in combination with very low benefit levels. The amount of national variation has been attributed to differences in level of economic growth, with Scandinavia leading, as well as to early social security traditions like the Bismarckian system in Germany, and to political developments like the long periods of social democratic rule in Scandinavia and the strength of the political right in Latin Europe (Esping-Andersen and Korpi 1984; Esping-Andersen 1990).

The "golden sixties" witnessed a fast rise in social security expenditure and other transfer payments. The "welfare state," referring to these transfer payments and to other fields of social policy like housing and state-provided or partly state-financed health care, seemed to have a bright future--until the 1974 oil crisis broke the spell. Since the second oil crisis national governments have been looking for means to reduce their budget deficits. The graying of the European population provides an additional incentive to lower old age benefits. At the same time employers are trying to reduce their contributions to social security, for instance by fighting illness absenteeism. Their example is Japan, where illness absenteeism is much lower, due in part to the greater degree of employee involvement, and social control, in the enterprise. Despite the setbacks, the term "welfare state" still has a very positive connotation in Europe. Almost all Western European countries still provide for extensive social security payments, including full-wage compensation in case of illness lasting for several weeks or even up to more than one year, followed by a lower compensation for another period. These kinds of transfer payments may be covered by law or by collective agreements, or by a combination of both. Additional enterprise social security or health care provisions have been rather unimportant since the extension of the welfare state in the 1960s. Most countries also possess some form of state-controlled health care for the lower income groups.

EMPLOYMENT AND EMPLOYMENT PROTECTION

Due to the rise of unemployment during the 1980s and 1990s, the focus of the "welfare state debate" has shifted from social security benefits to employment policies as the core of the welfare state. Employment policies encompass measures to increase the participation rate (the share of the adult population with a job or temporarily out of job) and measures to reduce unemployment. The former mainly refers to the participation rate of women, which has always been lower than that of men. The female participation rate has been highest in Scandinavia. The other Germanic countries and France are now catching up with Scandinavia, and they are followed by the other Latin countries.

With respect to unemployment, the line of division is a different one. While Norway and Sweden were able to keep unemployment below three percent until the 1990s, unemployment reached two-digit numbers in Denmark (also a Scandinavian country), Britain and the Low Countries. This rise popularized the idea that corporatism by itself did not have any effect on unemployment. An alternative explanation, referring to the existence of an explicit political commitment to full employment, was forwarded by Therborn. He juxtaposed the Swedish full employment policy with the Dutch course of high unemployment benefits and disability benefits, used for the same purpose, to facilitate economic restructuring. While Sweden, as well as other countries, had an explicit political commitment to full employment, Holland did not but gave high priority to compensating the effects of unemployment by high benefits (Therborn 1986, 1989). Others have pointed to the degree of centralization of collective bargaining, which is highest in Sweden and Norway, and which is a condition favoring an exchange of wage moderation and employment guarantees (Paloheimo 1990). Membership in the European Union has also been forwarded as an explanation. Until the mid-nineties Denmark was the only Scandinavian country in the European Union and, like the other member states, was hampered by its limits on economic intervention and labor market policies. However, except for the latter reference to the European Union, the yardsticks used to classify nations have been under attack. The Swiss position of low unemployment and limited centralization particularly defies any classification (Pekkarinen, Pohjola, and Rowthorn 1991; Soskice 1990). Indeed, there is hardly any link between the European models of labor relations, the level of unemployment, and unemployment policies. Moreover, in the 1990s unemployment has decreased to under ten percent in some of the high unemployment countries, and it is on the rise in other nations, like France.

Employment considerations are not only at the heart of national politics, employment protection as well as new jobs have also been bargaining topics by themselves. They are expressed in bargaining training facilities and protection against dismissal and layoff.

Employment guarantees at sector or enterprise level have become a regular bargaining issue since the 1980s. This "concessionary bargaining" involves union concessions like lower wage increase than in other sectors, a combination of working-time reduction and wage cuts, or even an extension of working time and cuts in real wages. The four-day work week at Volkswagen is a prominent example, but employment guarantees are currently being negotiated in almost all major European concerns. Many of them have been in trouble for some time and try to solve their problems by mass layoffs. In France and Italy the public sector has taken a leading role in providing employment guarantees, with strong government support. On the Continent unions often advocate training programs, in which they themselves may be involved, to improve worker mobility within the company. The German unions and works councils are most active in this field, as discussed in Chapter 7.

While trade unions are looking for enterprise and sector employment guarantees and propose concessions in return, employers are advocating a relaxation of dismissal and redundancy rules. They point to the need for greater flexibility in staffing the enterprise. Many firms are reluctant to hire new personnel in times of unstable economic conditions because of the strict rules on dismissal. According to employers, the strict rules may actually contribute to the expansion of temporary work contracts, especially for young workers. Indeed, protection against dismissal has been a union priority since World War II and in most countries it is well developed. National legislation imposes established procedures, in which the employer has to provide sufficient grounds for any dismissal: "serious" grounds in France; "objective" grounds in Sweden, with provisions for appeal by the workers involved. Since the rise of unemployment in the 1970s collective layoffs have been covered by rules as well. Recently, rules have been relaxed in a number of countries to meet the employer demands for greater flexibility. The procedures cover dismissal both for personal reasons and for economic reasons; only a few countries make a distinction between the two. A more important distinction is between individual dismissal and collective layoffs. The latter often require prior consultation with the works councils or the trade unions and a notice period ranging from one week to several months. The protection of clerical workers is generally more extensive than for manual workers, with longer notice periods.

The kind of rules pertaining to individual and collective dismissals differ along the lines of the three models of labor relations. In Great Britain and Ireland no statutory rules apply, but court rulings have established the obligation to consult the employee. In the Germanic model strict rules apply, either laid down in collective agreements, as in Scandinavia, or in law, as in the other nations. In some of them the works council has to be notified of all individual dismissals. Latin Europe relies even more on legislation. Spain and Portugal possess very extensive protection against dismissal, dating back to the period of fascist rule. Recent government attempts in both countries to bring these stringent rules more in line with those in Western Europe have met with fierce union opposition, including a nationwide Spanish strike in February 1994.

9

The European Union

Fifteen European nations make up the European Union. Although the European Union is primarily a common market--an economic union--it is also increasingly active in the field of social policy. Its main social accomplishments have been improvements in health and safety norms and in equal labor conditions for women.

A SHORT HISTORY

In 1950 French Foreign Minister Robert Schuman proposed one single international authority for the French and German coal and steel industries, the major economic bases of economic growth as well as of warfare. Like other forms of international cooperation--NATO for example--one of the aims was to integrate West Germany into Europe as an industrial power, as a means of preventing yet another major European conflict. The argument was that the opposite course, demanding huge war reparations, would impoverish Germany again and would refuel national resentment in that country, as had happened after World War I. Italy, Belgium, Holland and Luxemburg joined the initiative. The smaller nations especially needed an economically strong Germany as a market for their industrial produce and trade. The new institution, the Economic Coal and Steel Community, introduced in 1951 in a weaker version than originally planned, was also thought of as a first step towards fuller European unity. In 1957 the same six countries set up a more general European Economic Community (EEC), which overshadowed the Coal and Steel Community. It aimed at removing internal trade and customs barriers in order to promote the free flow of capital and labor within Europe to foster economic growth. Although the term EEC (or Common Market) was used until the early 1990s, the more recent term European Union (EU) will be applied here to the whole period.

The EU's first priority was agricultural policy, because of that sector's social and economic importance and the member states' lack of self-sufficiency. (At a later stage agricultural overproduction would become the main concern). Whatever social policy there was, was confined to the Coal and Steel Community. It consisted of promoting housing programs for steel workers and miners and of the European Social Fund, which financed the retraining and mobility of unemployed workers in both sectors. The Fund mainly served Germany, due to its large steel sector and to the fact that the Fund was financed through direct national contributions, of which Germany paid most. Since the Fund subsidized only governmental programs that had already been implemented, its effect was limited.

In the 1960s European social policy remained a marginal activity compared to economic policies, reflecting the strong economic growth during that decade and the concomitant rise in wages. The Coal and Steel Community displayed some activity in the form of reports on health and safety conditions in mining and the steel industry, later followed by EU reports on other sectors. It was not until the end of the 1960s that the international wave of social protest and rising unemployment in coal mining and steel companies, caused in part by continuous rationalization and reorganization, created pressure for more social policies. The widening of interest to social concerns was expressed in the adoption of a Social Action Programme in 1974. Its three main objectives were full employment, the improvement of working conditions and increased worker participation within the enterprise, as well as joint union-employer participation in EU decision making.

The first goal, full employment, was served by the expansion and activation of the Social Fund. No longer was it limited to subsidizing existing programs but it could also develop new programs. Moreover, after the expansion the Social Fund was financed out of the total EU budget instead of by direct national contributions, which made it more difficult for member states to demand as subventions the same amount they had contributed to the Fund. Increasingly, the poorer regions of Western Europe became the main beneficiaries, in accordance with the emergence of regional economic policies within the EU. The first oil crisis put the EU's efforts to reach the objective of full employment to the test. Indeed, new programs were developed in the by-now nine member states (Great Britain, Ireland and Denmark had just joined) but unemployment continued to rise, particularly after the second oil crisis. While some member states had two-digit unemployment figures, the lowest unemployment rates were found outside the EU, in Sweden and Switzerland, for example. This encouraged discussion on the effects of the EU as a possible factor contributing to unemployment by reducing the options for national social and economic policies.

The second objective, the improvement in labor conditions, was mainly served by directives on safety requirements and by comparative research on the situation in various industrial sectors. To promote such research, the EU set up the European Foundation for the Improvement of Living and Labour Conditions, based in Dublin. The concern for more equality in labor conditions also directed interest towards the position of immigrant workers. The EU tried to ensure equal treatment of the subjects of any member state in the other states, in order to encourage labor mobility. Most immigrants, however, came from outside the EU (North Africa, Turkey, former colonies), and their social position was weakened by the rise of unemployment in the 1980s.

The third objective, more worker participation, led to a number of initiatives--most of them abortive--to harmonize conditions on an advanced level of participation. Although direct efforts met with little success until 1994, national legislation was already adopted in a number of countries, and several multinational firms started introducing Europe-wide works councils.

The early 1980s was a period of general weariness with the EU. The second oil crisis made governments look for national solutions to the recession and to the free market. Conservative governments, inspired by Britain's Margaret Thatcher, abhorred the EU's "bureaucratic" rule making and its "uncontrolled" spending as barriers to economic growth. However, two-thirds of the budget was still spent on agriculture to guarantee minimum prices to farmers under conditions of overproduction.

In 1985 the member states decided to complete the single unified market by the end of 1992. A new wave of EU enthusiasm swept Western Europe, later fueled by the demise of the Russian domination of Central Europe. The year 1992 became the deadline for the abolition of non-tariff trade barriers. It also unleashed intense activities in the field of monetary and economic policies. An additional agreement intended to do away with all border checks between most of the member states.

A single European market not only had its positive side. A possible social effect might be "social dumping," in the form of a shift of investment and employment from the richer member states to the socially less developed southern European nations. Another result could be increasing policy competition between equally developed countries aimed at reducing labor costs. In order to reduce these fears, the member states adopted a "Social Charter" of fundamental employees' rights in 1989--except for Great Britain, which did not want to comply with new international social standards. The Charter was followed by the elaborate Social Action Programme, at a time in which economic conditions hardly favored any new social measures, however (Lange 1993). The new step towards a unified Europe was sealed in the early 1990s by the Treaty, concluded in the Dutch town of Maastricht, to go forward to a full economic and monetary union, with a common currency. The EU laid down a number of minimum conditions to be fulfilled by the member states that wanted to join the monetary union, referring to the rate of inflation, the size of the national debt and the percentage of state deficit. In the same period three new members were admitted -- Austria, Finland, and Sweden. Currently, only four Western European countries (Iceland, Malta, Norway, and Switzerland) remain outside the scope of the EU.

TRADE UNIONS AND EMPLOYERS

The "Council of Ministers"--consisting of the national ministers of economic, social or other affairs, depending upon the issues at hand--make the final decisions about EU policies. The decisions are prepared by the European Commission, seated in Brussels. Its former chairman, the French Socialist Jacques Delors, played an important role in the adoption of the Social Charter. The European parliament, elected in direct elections in the member states, has limited influence. The Commission is advised by the Economic and Social Committee (Ecosoc), in which trade unions and employers predominate, although farmers and consumers' organizations are represented as well. Its sheer size, 189 members, and its composition contribute to its lack of influence.

Trade union and employer involvement in European decision making does not imply that they have always been in favor of European unification. On both sides the attitudes have varied over time and have often been a mixture of negative and positive feelings. French employers were among the early advocates of a European social policy because of the relatively high French wages and social expenditure in the 1950s. In their view, economic competition within a unified market would require a harmonization of all social expenditure. The opposite view, advocated by the German government and supported by most employers' confederations won. This view defended non-intervention in social policies in order not to disturb the functioning of the market and the relationship between unions and employers. The trade unions were divided. Some of them favored an upward harmonization of wages and social expenditures to the highest national level; others were more reluctant to give up the advantage of being a low-cost country. These positions did not necessarily overlap with a pro- or anti-EU stand. The French CGT, for instance, has always advocated upward leveling of labor conditions, but rejected the EU as a device to promote the mobility of international capital. Dutch unions, involved in a strict state wage policy during the 1950s and 1960s, supported European integration because of the new markets it would open, but wanted to retain their low-wage advantage. The opposition against the EU as a capitalist instrument favoring international capital at the expense of the workers' interests has not been a monopoly of the communist-dominated unions like the CGT. Several social democratic parties and union confederations have opposed or at least mistrusted the EU for a long time, because of the lack of social policies to complement its economic impact. This view was very prevalent in Great Britain, where the Labour Party (backed by the unions) made the "No to Europe" a political issue in elections.

In the course of the 1980s there was a general shift in attitude among trade unions and social democrats (including the Labour Party) that had been at most lukewarm until then. They now see the advantages of European-wide social policies, if only because they have not been able to reach any social improvement in national politics. This growing agreement has allowed the European unions to engage more actively in the so-called "Social Dialogue". Most national governments support this development because social talks at the European level would supposedly reduce the claims put to them. Even the more conservative governments back them, if only because the expected union-employer disagreement would prevent any new extension of social policy, just as back home. The employers have long been able to block efforts, by arguing that they are too divided among themselves to develop a common point of view, because of the large differences between national and sectoral conditions and even between companies.

Since the adoption of the Social Charter in 1989 the Social Dialogue has become a more active one (Rhodes 1991). Its position has been formalized in the Maastricht Treaty. The Council of Ministers and the European Commission are now obliged to consult the "social partners" in the course of any new European legislation, as laid down in the Social Action Programme. At the same time the role of the national governments has been slightly weakened, since draft directives in the field of health and safety conditions no longer require a unanimous vote by the Council of Ministers, but rather a qualified majority (as a means to bypass the British obstruction of European social policy). The social partners are divided about the direction the Social Dialogue should take, however. Most trade unions consider it a first step towards regular consultation, a form of tripartism. Moreover, they also see it as a forum for Europe-wide negotiations on framework agreements. Such agreements could then be declared binding on all member states by the European Commission. Europe-wide bargaining is still a long way off, however. In a number of industrial sectors European sector organizations exist at both sides, but their talks have not yet reached the stage of bargaining on labor conditions (Bercusson 1993). One of the sectors moving in that direction is the construction industry, where talks have focused on the evasion of national wage and social security regulations by posting mock "self-employed" British construction workers, especially in Germany. Generally the employers hold off this kind of Europe-wide industry bargaining, pointing to the international trend towards decentralization and increased flexibility. On the other hand, they also see the rationale for concluding such agreements as a possible safeguard against greater European intervention in the economy by means of legislation. A number of national employers' confederations, including the British CBI, reject all European bargaining. They do not want any European social activity, or anything that might lead to "corporatist structures".

Does the Social Dialogue, indeed, point to a development towards corporatism? As to the organizations involved in the Social Dialogue, they are still weakly developed. The European Trade Union Confederation, ETUC, was formed in the 1950s by the national peak organizations. Originally a regional subdivision of the International Confederation of Free Trade Unions, it became an independent institution in 1972, admitting Catholic as well as communist-dominated union confederations. It now coordinates all major national trade union confederations, not only within the European Union but throughout Western

Europe and Turkey. The only exception is the CGT, which has long been a member of the rival international communist organization for trade unions, dominated by the Russian communists. It has never applied for ETUC membership and its application would have been treated with mistrust by the social democratic and the Catholic ETUC members. The ETUC has often been plagued by internal discord among confederations representing and defending different models of labor relations. In particular the TUC and the German DGB, the latter being by far the most powerful ETUC member, have opposed each other with respect to the need for Europe-wide bargaining and the degree of compliance that could be imposed upon their own membership. Recently, the internal organization of the ETUC has been reinforced to meet the needs of the Social Dialogue. Its social partner, the Union of Industrial and Employers' Confederations in Europe, UNICE, was not formed until the start of the EU in 1958. At least in its formal statements it has shown less internal disagreement, but that accomplishment has been reached by defending the position of the most outspoken free market defenders and anti-Europeans, in other words, by just saying "no" all the time. Lately it has become more cooperative, however, even forwarding proposals of its own (Carley 1993).

The influence of the European organizations seems unevenly divided so far. The ETUC recently was able to put some issues on the agenda, but the outcome often has been more in line with what UNICE had in mind than with the original union proposals. This also has to do with the internal disagreement within the ETUC, however. Several features are missing to make this kind of contacts into corporatism (Henley and Tsakalotos 1992). First, the organizational structure of a number of participating European trade union and employers' confederations, including the DGB, does not provide them with the power to commit their member organizations. A unified European government, that is able to conclude agreements with both the employers and the unions is also missing (Schmitter and Streeck 1991). Moreover, the idea of social partnership may be prevalent in Germanic countries but it is still hardly developed in Latin Europe.

THE EU IMPACT ON LABOR CONDITIONS

Leaving aside the indirect effects on economic growth and growth-related wages and employment, the European Union has had a modest impact on labor conditions. The direct effects are reached by European "advice" and by "directives." The latter form a kind of European legislation and have to be integrated in the national legislation of the member states. This European social legislation has given rise to political debate along two lines of division. First, countries that do already comply with European standards try to enhance the norms to their own level in order to safeguard their economic position, while countries that have lower norms try to keep them at that level with the same goal in mind. In working conditions a line of division exists between the Germanic countries--under German leadership--and France as leaders, versus Southern Europe (that is, the rest of Latin Europe) and sometimes also Great Britain as followers. On several occasions the German government, employers and unions have spoken out at against the danger of social dumping. Indeed, this is more a threat to the industry-based German economy than to the more service-oriented economies of France and the smaller nations like Holland and Belgium. Germany's leading position has been negatively affected, however, by German reunification, which has provided the country with outdated and highly unsafe industries in the former communist eastern regions. The second line of division is between countries that possess extensive and detailed social legislation, such as France and Germany, and countries where regulation is left to industrial organizations or to joint union-employer institutions. This culture of self-regulation is especially prevalent in Britain, as part of the British voluntarism in social and economic matters, and in Scandinavia, where it finds its expression in joint union-employer agreements.

These differences in legal systems cause delays in the integration of European directives within the existing bodies of legal rules, and sometimes they defy any attempt at more uniformity, in particular in the field of social security. They also constitute a reason to oppose regulations from "Brussels". Southern European opposition is based on its low standards, Danish opposition on its self-regulation and British opposition on a combination of both low standards (though not in all working conditions) and dislike of social legislation. Increasingly, however, the European Commission is trying to circumvent such opposition by stimulating self-regulation by national or international sector organizations. This self-regulation by the organizations involved and by the national governments under EU pressure is now deemed more effective than a top-down approach. It has been dubbed "subsidiarity". It is interesting that this term has been popularized by the Catholic social doctrine as the basis of traditional Catholic corporatism. According to that ideology sector organizations (together with the unions in case of social affairs) should handle their own sector affairs and set their own standards in order to avoid state control. In the EU it now also refers to national activities rather than Euro-wide regulation.

Related to the start of European integration in coal mining and the steel industry in the 1950s, one of the early fields of European regulation was health and safety conditions at the workplace. Since the mid-1980s general directives have been issued to deal with worker exposure to chemical, physical, and biological agents; the operation and maintenance of machines and work tools; noise at work, and work at computer screens (James 1993). The debate on such issues prompted a number of countries to adapt their legislation in the course of the 1970s. Since the promulgation of EU directives the member states are under constant pressure to make new changes. The effect has been a general uplifting of work conditions in Western Europe. Moreover, the future of European concern with health and safety looks bright. Unanimity is no longer required in this field, there is some agreement about the need to improve health and safety conditions, and, with the exception of the nuclear power stations, unhealthy industries are gradually losing importance in the European economies.

A topic which has received wider publicity, without result so far, has been the regulation of working time, an issue of conflict not so much between nations as between unions and employers. Not all European unions share the high priority given by the German trade unions to a thirty-five hour working week. As a consequence, the ETUC has hardly been able to reach a common view, in contrast to UNICE, which opposes any European initiative on this point. Even a compromise of forty-eight hours as a maximum, far in excess of the actual weekly working time, has given rise to protests from Britain and the poorer member states since it would affect the living standards of those willing to make more hours. In general the division here has remained one of the richer continental states, with German as the most outspoken proponent of a European measure, versus the poorer nations and Great Britain (the British government and British industry, not the TUC this time). In this field, the odds are against any future regulation because of the increasing flexibility in working time, with long working weeks in exchange for longer holidays as one of the options.

Arguably the best European record is in gender equality, with a number of directives of a more principal nature. The European activities in this field have been favorably influenced by the fighting spirit of the international women's movement, international initiatives in the United Nations and the International Labor Organization (ILO) and by the fact that no country dares publicly oppose this equality. The original pressure came from the French government and employers, fearing for their competitive power, but it was not until the mid-1970s that the first directive was issued--on wage equality for work of equal value. This left intact the separation between men occupying the well-paid functions and women doing the lower paid work. The measure had more impact on the Continent, in particular in countries with centralized bargaining, than in Britain, with its tradition of decentralized bargaining (Rubery 1992). Later directives extended the fight against this line of division by demanding equal opportunities to enter the labor process, equal opportunities for vocational training and equal treatment regarding labor conditions and social security. The EU has also promoted positive action in favor of women, patterned after the American example of "affirmative action" (Cox 1993).

Although most states already possess laws on equality and non-discrimination, they have been lived up to only in Scandinavia because of the social democrats' encouragement of female access to the labor market, including higher echelon functions. The directives have encouraged women's demands for equal treatment and have also stimulated the mostly male-dominated unions to become active in the field. In most member states the issue has been on the political agenda for some time. The equal treatment of women in social security has been a particularly hot issue since most national systems of social security are family-oriented, offering better income maintenance provisions for male breadwinners than for other workers. As a consequence, adaptation of the systems of social security has been a costly affair in some countries.

As soon as European guidelines become more detailed, disagreement often delays or prevents regulation. An example is maternity leave. Despite the fact that it is considered a working condition for which no unanimity is required, it has taken a long time to issue a directive. Again, the line of division has been one between the northern continental states, including France, and the poorer states and Britain. The original draft proposed one hundred percent compensation, as is usual in Germany and the smaller nations, but later drafts reduced it to eighty percent, then ended up at the same level as sickness compensation--with a minimum of seventy-five percent.

In the mid-1990s the European Union became a scapegoat for the international cuts in social security spending. A number of governments defended such measures by referring to the need to meet the conditions of the future monetary union, like the French government did at the end of 1995--the start of the large public sector strikes.

EUROPEAN WORKS COUNCILS

While gender equality predominantly has been a political affair, handled by the national governments, unions and employers have focused on yet another area: worker participation. This has been an issue since the mid-1970s, when the wave of legislation and agreements affected most European countries. The original proposals aimed specifically at workers in multinational companies who increasingly lost their influence because of the internationalization of companies. For that reason the early drafts applied only to international companies with plants or subsidiaries of over fifty employees in at least two member states. Uniform rules about such a "European works council" were rejected, however, under pressure from national governments and employers. Still, the European discussion on worker participation influenced some of the member states to adapt their own legislation. The French Auroux legislation was one of the examples, aiming at raising France to "European" levels in this respect.

In the course of the 1980s the European works council remained an issue in "Brussels," but the idea of a uniform European type was left for a framework directive which would be complementary to national legislation. In the early 1990s a new draft directive was framed for "European companies," that is, companies with over one thousand employees and/or with subsidiaries or plants of over one hundred employees in at least two member states. Management and workers' representatives would have to negotiate the nature and competence of the European works council in such companies; in case of lasting disagreement the rules of the company's country of origin would apply. This proposal was rejected by UNICE, which drafted its own "advice," rather than a directive. Employers, hardly willing to bargain with trade unions on an international scale, have pointed to the time-consuming and costly nature of transnational worker participation. The trade union movement has also been highly divided, with clashes between the ETUC's two largest members, the TUC and the DGB. The German unions want to impose strict guidelines more or less conforming to the German system in order to prevent "participation dumping" (*Mitbestimmungsflucht*) to nations with less worker participation, as a corollary of social dumping. They also advocate open entry to the councils for unorganized workers in order to enhance their legitimacy. The TUC, used to worker participation in the form of shop stewards, prefers to ban non-union members.

In September 1994 the member states finally accepted a directive on European Works councils, with the exception of Great Britain. The directive applies to companies with over one thousand employees which are active in at least two member states. Within two years it must be integrated in national legislation and have the force of law. In that two-year period companies and unions may introduce any form of Euro-wide worker participation on a voluntary base. After that period all companies are obliged to engage in negotiations with trade unions aiming at the establishment of a Euro-works council. The negotiations must result in a written agreement, but the model of the Euro-works council is still a matter of free choice. Only in cases companies have not introduced such a council before September 1999 will they have to follow a uniform model for the Euro-works council. That council is comprised of employee representatives from all nations involved. Representatives will meet annually and have information rights and the right of advice in matters affecting the company's workforce.

Prior to the passing of the directive in September 1994 over thirty large companies had already introduced some form of Euro works councils, or more specific, some form of Euro-wide worker consultation. Most of them were established in automobile manufacture and in the machine and chemical industries, in which the production processes are often internationally integrated. French enterprises have been among the pioneers. This may appear surprising in view of the nature of French labor relations, but one of the motives has been to promote the hierarchical internal organization of French companies among the foreign subsidiaries. An additional motive is the opportunity to bypass the French unions and do business with Germanic unions. Even some British multinationals have introduced European forms of worker consultation, despite the fact that the obligation does not apply to that country.

The early and voluntary European works councils or similar initiatives differ in composition. Some consist of company employees; others leave the unions a free hand to compose their own delegation. The councils do not possess any formal power. Rather, the union-employer agreements speak about a company social dialogue or about an exchange of views, without any obligation for the employer to follow formal consultation procedures or to implement the outcome of the "dialogue" (Gold and Hall 1992). The major exception is Volkswagen, which in 1992 introduced a Europe-wide consultation procedure, the first of its kind in Europe. Most multinational companies are still without any form of European worker participation and are actually involved in the process of

decentralization, discussed in Chapter 7 (Marginson et al. 1993). The EU efforts
have encouraged international contacts between unions and works councils in the
various subsidiaries of such companies and contacts between sector unions in
general. The unions are still a long way from developing common standpoints,
however.

CONVERGENCE OR DIVERGENCE?

There has been some discussion about whether the impact of the European
Union on the national systems of labor relations will lead to convergence (Henley
and Tsakalotos 1992; Due, Madsen, Jensen 1991). Most authors point to the large
differences in national institutions, legal rules, bargaining patterns, conflict
traditions and government involvement. The institutions are an expression of a
wide variation in national and even regional political and social culture. Neither
European Directives nor national legislation aimed at adopting European
standards has reduced the great national variations and the differences between
British, Germanic and Latin labor relations. Germanic sector bargaining has
certainly functioned as a model for Latin labor relations, but a major effect of the
Auroux reforms in France has been to promote enterprise-level activities rather
than sector bargaining, and in Italy the role of sector bargaining continues to be
affected by the high level of local union militancy. National agreements fail to
keep in check this kind of spontaneous grassroots action, and European directives
will not fare better. The same applies to Britain, where the informal shop floor
strikes provide the national government with an argument to reject any kind of
European interference in British labor relations since that would only reinforce
the unions' position. In turn, the British choice of a low-wage strategy will widen
the gap in labor conditions with Germany and other Germanic countries, which
have adopted training-oriented labor relations.

The differences are to some extent the outcome of great variations in labor and
employer power. In the 1980s labor's power was negatively affected by adverse
economic and sometimes also unfavorable political conditions, but weakened
labor does not necessarily lead to convergence. Both Scandinavia and countries
with weaker labor movements like Holland and France have witnessed this
development. The Germanic labor movements seem to weather the storms better
than their British and Latin counterparts, but this actually increases the existing
divergence in collective bargaining and trade union power rather than leading to
a convergence of the three models.

Another important current trend, decentralization, need not lead to convergence
either, since it does not affect the labor relations models to the same degree. To
some extent it undermines the possible trend towards convergence which might
result from the internationalization of the economy. Rather than imposing their
own national systems of labor relations, multinationals often leave their
subsidiaries a free hand to deal with the unions. Moreover, the effects of

decentralization are completely different in the Germanic and the Latin models, as has been shown for Germany and Italy. More flexibility in labor conditions and labor relations could also lead to a greater diversity between and within nations.

Probably the major factor contributing to convergence consists of the minimum conditions imposed by the European Union and especially affecting the poorer member states. The effect of the EU's social policies have been limited, however, except for a few issues like health and safety conditions and gender equality. A second development might be a Europe-wide form of pattern bargaining, with IG Metall in a pioneering role. This kind of bargaining has already existed for some time, but it does not seem to be expanding. Even in countries like Holland, which traditionally have been dependent on the German economy, the German pattern set by the IG Metall has not always been followed. In a number of cases union priorities in the smaller nations have been completely different from those in Germany. Although the Euro-works councils may also serve as catalysts of convergence (and of international bargaining), their importance has been limited because of the low frequency of meetings, the emphasis on employment issues which divide rather than unite the national unions and works councils, and the general trend toward decentralization.

For a long time to come, Europe will continue to be a patchwork of nation states with national systems of labor relations. Only with great difficulty can they be grouped together into a British, a Germanic and a Latin model in order to show common European trends as well as major European cleavages.

10

Five Pairs of Nations

After the extensive references to the larger countries in the previous chapters, this chapter compares five pairs of smaller nations. The aim of this comparison is a discussion of some of the more subtle national differences within the Germanic and the Latin group rather than a complete picture of these nations. Subtle though the differences may be, to the inhabitants of the countries involved they fully justify the distinction of a national model of labor relations.

DENMARK AND NORWAY

Both Denmark and Norway are small countries in terms of population size: Denmark has 5.2 million inhabitants, Norway 4.2 million. However, a look at the map reveals great contrasts in size and landscape. While Denmark is a small, low and flat country, Norway consists of a 1,200-mile mountain range, interrupted by the famous fjords. This variation in landscape has given rise to different economic structures. The Norwegian economy has always heavily relied on shipping and fishing. Its small industrial sector is based on hydro-electrical energy, and recently the country has become an important gas and oil producer. A large part of this energy sector is in public hands. Denmark is a major exporter of dairy products. Small and craft-based enterprises predominate in industry, in which public enterprise is a marginal phenomenon.

Despite the contrasts, both countries share, along with Sweden, a common Scandinavian system of politics and labor relations, including the strong position of social democrats in national politics. They are Protestant countries in which neither religion nor language are political issues. They also have in common a long tradition of corporatism and nationwide all-industry wage bargaining, large social democratic union confederations and well-developed welfare states without much overt conflict.

In Scandinavia the so-called Basic Agreements, which are regularly updated, contain the basic rules of labor relations. Labor legislation is not very extensive and because of the tradition of all-industry wage bargaining, setting annual or biannual frameworks for sector negotiations, the national government is not heavily involved in wage negotiations. In Norway wage policies have been confined to the immediate postwar years and the period after the first oil crisis. They mainly consisted of imposing compulsory arbitration, almost a trademark of Norwegian labor relations. On several occasions between 1950 and the mid-1970s compulsory arbitration was imposed on sector organizations, but only three times on the peak organizations. Denmark's wage bargaining has been somewhat less centralized most of the time. The national government has been more actively involved, but in some cases its role has been limited to enforcing compliance with central wage agreements concluded by the peak organizations. During most of the 1960s and early 1970s the national governments also presented a macro-economic framework for wage bargaining, which gave parameters rather than strict guidelines, however. Since the mid-1970s Danish government intervention has also been stricter than in Norway. One of the instruments used has been a fixed ceiling to price compensation. Strikes are not very frequent, and strike figures covering a number of years may easily overrate the strike propensity, especially in Denmark. In that country there are hardly any strikes most of the time, but this period of almost complete labor peace is interrupted once a decade by a year in which the whole country seems to be on strike, as in 1973 and 1985.

In addition to this variation in state intervention, the countries differ in union structure. Most member unions of the dominant Norwegian union confederation, *Landsorganisasjonen* (LO) are industrial unions. Indeed, related to the late rise of trade unions, the country has been one of the pioneers in industrial unionism. Denmark's trade unionism is much older, and it was the first country on the European continent to develop trade unions--in the form of craft workers' organizations--later complemented by separate general workers' unions. Currently, Denmark is the only Continental country in which craft unionism has survived. However, the smaller number of organizations and the strong coordinating power of the major confederations (also called LO) form a contrast with British craft unionism and position the country firmly in the Germanic group. Moreover, general unions now dominate within the Danish LO. In Norway and Denmark the LO mainly appeals to manual workers and public sector workers. In both countries a separate confederation, which is smaller and less politically committed, addresses clerical workers and public sector employees. In a typical Scandinavian form of pattern bargaining, the smaller confederations leave all-industry bargaining to the LO and the major employer confederations, however, and adopt the results for their own members. The Norwegian membership rate is under sixty percent, well below the Danish rate of eighty percent. The difference is due to the union involvement in unemployment insurance in the latter country and to the greater interest of the Danish unions in worker participation. In both countries the major employers' peak organization, which acts as the LO's bargaining partner, is also primarily rooted in industry, and less so or not at all in commercial services, where smaller employers' confederations exist. The membership rate of organizations on the employers' side is low. The members of the major Danish confederation employ no more than about one-quarter of the industrial workforce.

The Danish unions have always highly favored worker participation. A permanent and joint employer-union cooperation committee (*Samarbejdsvaevnet*) solves conflicts between the union representatives and employers. The Norwegian unions have been much less interested in worker participation, due to the preponderant role of the public sector and possibly also to the predominance of the commercial services sector. The difference is reflected in the number of union competencies listed in the Basic Agreements. The Norwegian social democratic party has at times been a major advocate of worker participation in the form of co-determination, but it withdrew a co-determination proposal in the 1950s in response to lack of union interest. In the 1960s the country became a pioneer in "Cooperation Projects," which tried to introduce group work. Even this initiative was based primarily on scientific interest, in particular of the socio-technical management school of the Tavistock Institute. It was not until the mid-1970s that the Norwegian unions showed more interest, but they did not follow the Danish (and Swedish) example of workers' funds.

Apart from unemployment (over ten percent in Denmark during most of the 1980s and now up to seven percent in Norway) major recent issues are the close link between the two national LOs and the social democratic parties, the structure of trade unionism and the prospects for nationwide bargaining.

In both countries the LO is intimately linked with the social democratic party, which has more success in Norway than in Denmark. In Norway the party has dominated national politics and the national government most of the time since 1935; in Denmark it has been compelled to form coalition cabinets and was out of power during the 1980s. The fate of the parties has encouraged the discussion on the union-party relationship. The parties are eager to appeal to clerical workers and non-union members, while the major union confederations try to appeal to non-socialist voters. Despite some minor adaptations in common union-party bodies, the union-party link remains a very intimate one, both formally and informally.

The trade union structure has been a topic for quite some time. Proposals have been forwarded to amalgamate the existing member organizations (over twenty-five in both countries) into a small number of cartels or large sector unions. The Norwegian proposal leaves only four cartels (state employees, municipal workers, industry, and services), and a Danish project advocates a reduction of the number of LO member unions to nine. The larger member unions strenuously oppose the plans, however. Meanwhile, Danish employers have engaged in a fast process of amalgamation within the major confederations, which has reduced the number of member organizations from 150 to 30. One of the purposes of this reorganization is to reduce the number of collective agreements to a couple of multi-sector agreements, leaving the enterprises and the local unions greater latitude in bargaining. This development towards larger sector and multi-sector agreements raises the question about the future of nationwide peak agreements. In particular employers regularly voice doubts about the use of this annual or biannual ritual, but at the appointed time rejoin the LO at the bargaining table as a means to enforce wage restraint.

BELGIUM AND HOLLAND

Belgium and Holland have much in common. They are small, predominantly flat and aptly called the "Low Countries." Both are densely populated. Belgium has ten million inhabitants and Holland (officially named The Netherlands) fifteen million, which makes it the most populous of the smaller European nations. The Belgian and Dutch national economies are based on export-oriented industries, large service sectors, and transit trade to Germany, handled by the major ports--Rotterdam in Holland and Antwerp in Belgium. During most of the twentieth century national politics has been dominated by Christian Democrats, in coalition either with conservative liberals or social democrats. Extensive social policies contributed to high state deficits in the 1980s, which have continued to be a major government concern, in combination with the rise of unemployment to over ten percent.

An important difference in economic structure is the traditional domination of the Belgian economy (more specific, Wallony, the French-speaking part of Belgium) by steel works and coal mining, partly in the hands of national banks. The Dutch economy is more service oriented, and its industry is dominated by a few multinationals. A political difference is the prevalence of the language issue in Belgium, which has recently been federalized into a French-speaking part, a Dutch-speaking part (Flanders) and the bilingual capital, Brussels. A second political and cultural difference is in religion. Belgium is a Catholic country, with a strong current of "anti-clericalism" in Wallony. Holland is a Protestant country with a sizable Catholic minority. Together they form the Dutch Christian Democratic Party, but the Protestants dominate Dutch national culture.

Corporatism, the combination of sector and company bargaining, the fragmentation of the union movement along religious and status lines, and worker participation by means of works councils are common features of labor relations in the Low Countries. However, they vary in the nature of corporatism, in government involvement in wage bargaining and in trade union strength.

As a counterpart to the Dutch Social and Economic council (SER), Belgium has two separate councils, one to discuss economic issues and a more important one for social affairs "National Labor Council" (*Nationale Arbeidsraad*, NAR/ *Conseil national du travail*, CNT). This social council NAR/CNT is used for corporatist contacts with the national government and also to conclude nationwide all-industry agreements covering specific labor condition like holidays and worker participation. Over forty such "interprofessional" agreements have been concluded since 1868, when this tradition started. In Holland all-industry bargaining does not take place in the SER, but in a joint union-employer institution, the Foundation of Labor. Invariably, Dutch all-industry bargaining has failed, however, or has resulted in declarations of intent which should serve as guiding principles for sector wage bargaining. Holidays and worker participation are often laid down in laws. The Belgian interprofessional agreements are more akin to the Scandinavian system of employer-union regulation of labor relations, while the Dutch system resembles the German preference for legislation.

Two other characteristics reinforce this difference. First, as in Scandinavia, corporatist contacts in Belgium regularly take place on an informal basis. While the top Dutch union and employer leaders are members of the Dutch SER, the top Belgian leaders do not assist at meetings of the Belgian NAR/CNT, which leaves room for informal peak-level contacts outside the council. This reinforces the position of the peak organizations vis-à-vis the national government. In contrast, one-third of the seats in the Dutch SER are occupied by prominent outside experts, who take an active part in the discussions and are highly influential.

The second difference is the heavy Dutch state involvement in collective bargaining. Until the first oil crisis the two countries were almost opposites in that respect. While the Belgian government ended its involvement in the late 1940s, the Dutch government continued a "guided wage policy," which set very strict limits for sector bargaining. The unions and employers' associations were intimately involved in the formation and the implementation of that statutory wage policy. The guidelines were based on their advice and on econometric data supplied by the national Planning Office, whose head is one of the independent experts in the SER. The wage policy ended in the late 1960s, due to a tight labor market which gave rise to illegal "black wages." After the mid-1970s both governments interfered in wage bargaining; in the 1990s peak-level "guidelines for moderation" and "declarations of intent" have explicitly prevented any new intervention in both countries. The variation in corporatism and in wage policies shows an interesting contrast between the kind of pragmatism that exists in the two countries: informal bargaining in Belgium and reference to econometric data about the country's world market position in Holland, probably due to its long-standing tradition as a nation of international trade rather than industry.

The difference in state involvement is also linked to variation in union strength. The Belgian unions have enjoyed a strong base in heavy industry and mining, centers of French-inspired *action directe*, which has kept the social democrats from participation in wage policies in order not to lose their grassroots support. In combination with the union administration of unemployment funds in Belgium, the strong grassroots support and Belgian union priority of strong locals may explain the difference in union density, which is twice as high in

Belgium (over sixty percent) as in Holland. In Holland, with its economic tradition of trade rather than industry, the trade unions have lacked such a base and have mainly been interested in sector and all-industry organizations. At the end of World War II in a "Great Exchange," they even traded in union involvement within the enterprise for their participation in the SER. The low rate in Holland has not affected the strength of corporatism, but it has urged the unions to look for government support of labor conditions in the form of legislation and has tied them to wage policies. The strike rate is also much lower in Holland than in Belgium (Hancké and Slomp 1996).

In both countries the union movement has been split. In Belgium the Catholic union confederation is even larger than the social democratic one, and they are flanked by a small liberal union movement and a new "cadre" union federation. The much smaller Dutch union movement has been even more fragmented, with a social democratic and a Catholic federation (merged in the 1970s), a Protestant organization and two confederations mainly addressing private and public sector "cadre."

Worker participation differs in accordance with the variation in union strength and the union priorities. As in Scandinavia, the Belgian union representatives play a key role in worker participation, both within and outside the statutory works councils. The Dutch councils, more in line with the German tradition, are rather formally independent from the trade unions and have long been neglected by them. The unions used to treat them as a potential rival movement rather than as a network of potential members.

In both countries the discussion about the decentralization of labor relations has been going on for some time. Although the actual impact of the process of decentralization is rather limited, the Dutch unions are affected most, due to their weak position within the enterprises.

AUSTRIA AND SWITZERLAND

Although Austria and Switzerland are both small and mountainous, these Alpine countries do not have much in common. Austria, with 7.7 million inhabitants, is the remnant of the Austrian Empire, with the imperial city of Vienna as a grossly oversized capital. This German-speaking country has long struggled to define its place in Europe and its relationship with Germany. The Christian Democratic party, dominated by Catholics and strongly represented in the countryside, and the social democrats, whose stronghold is in the capital, compete for power and occasionally build coalition governments. In contrast, Switzerland, with 6.9 million inhabitants, is an old and self-conscious republic, one of the few countries not directly affected by the two world wars. Its politics have traditionally been highly decentralized and concentrated in the cantons. This has proved to be a highly effective means to de-politicize the differences in languages (German, French, Italian) and even more in religion (Catholics and

Protestants). Whatever the election outcomes, the major parties are always represented in government.

Austria is a full-fledged welfare state with a large public sector, which has served to keep unemployment low by absorbing the unemployed. Switzerland is often either praised or despised as the last proud vestige of unbridled capitalism. Its economy is dominated by multinationals producing technologically advanced products and by international banking. The country spends much less on social policies, but it has kept unemployment low by putting strict limits on permanent labor immigration, in particular from Italy. In labor relations four differences stand out, the nature of corporatism and collective bargaining, the degree of government involvement and legal regulation, the types of organizations involved and the extent of worker participation within the enterprise (Katzenstein 1984).

Even more than Scandinavia, Austria still stands as the most prominent example of corporatism. Wage bargaining by the sector organizations, as well as social and economic state policies, are discussed in the "Joint Commission for Price and Wage Issues" (*Paritätische Kommission für Preis- und Lohnfragen*). It has three subcommittees--one for wages, one for prices and one for general social and economic issues. In contrast to the Dutch SER it is an informal institution with no secretariat or an office of its own. In the Joint Committee two employers' organizations are represented, one statutory "Chamber" organizing industry and services and a second one for agriculture. The chambers, whose membership is compulsory, are a traditional corporatist device dating from the period of Catholic-inspired fascism in the mid-1930s. Labor is also represented by two organizations: the social democratic trade union confederation, the only one in the country, and a "Labor Chamber," an independent body structured along territorial rather than sectoral lines with compulsory membership for all dependent wage earners, public employees exempted. The Joint Committee is an independent institution, but there are strong links with the national government. The Chancellor (prime minister) presides over its sessions, and cabinet ministers assist at the Committee's meetings. As a consequence, the borderline between the participating organizations and the national government has become blurry.

The Committee, or more specific, the subcommittee on wages, discusses the wage claims forwarded by the unions, and it has to approve the start of any new round of negotiations. Although this could provide the Committee with a large influence on collective bargaining, beginning in the 1980s its approval has more and more become a rubber stamp. On both sides the umbrella organizations strongly coordinate sector bargaining, however.

In Switzerland corporatism is weakly developed, although there are informal meetings between the national government and the peak organizations. Collective bargaining is decentralized, more so than in any other Germanic country. It takes place at the level of a canton or a number of cantons and is monitored only to some extent by the umbrella organizations. When nationwide sector agreements are concluded, they leave ample room for regional, local and company bargaining. Even in the small public sector most wage bargaining is decentralized because of the country's all-pervading federal structure--a contrast with Austria, despite the fact that the latter is also formally a federal system.

The Swiss government has never interfered with wage bargaining. In the informal peak-level talks in that country pay issues have never been an important topic. This government abstention is rivalled only by Germany's legal guarantee of *Tarifautonomie*, but Switzerland does not possess any law to enforce it. This is in conformity with the more general lack of labor legislation. While Austria possesses extensive legal rules on various aspects of labor relations, more or less comparable to Germany, the Swiss system is one of voluntary cooperation and compliance with agreements. Only some labor conditions are enforced by law. This kind of voluntary regulation may show some superficial resemblance with the Scandinavian labor relations, but there is a major difference in trade union strength and in the union role in society.

Switzerland has the lowest unionization rate of the Germanic countries, under thirty percent, half the Austrian rate. One explanation of this difference is the monopoly position of one trade union organization in Austria, strongly linked to the powerful social democratic party, and the division of the labor movement in Switzerland along religious and status lines.

As opposed to the virtual cooperation between unions and employers in Austria (in that respect this country shows more resemblance with Scandinavia), the Swiss system is one of union compliance with employer demands--a union "understanding" of the needs of the free market. In terms of conflict the result is the same: both countries have the lowest strike rate in Europe. In Anglo-Saxon terms Austria might be called a "union firm" and Switzerland a "non-union firm" with a highly developed system of Human Resource Management (an "HRM-firm").

The difference in union strength and in cooperation versus compliance is also expressed in the nature of worker participation. The Austrian system has the same roots as the German one, the revolutionary upheaval after World War I, and it is similar to that system. The Austrian union movement has also shared the German neglect of workplace issues during most of the postwar period, but it has not been punished with a low union density. The Swiss do not really have a system of worker representation. Efforts to implement a legal framework in the 1970s were defeated in a referendum, like so many other kinds of social legislation. Many of the larger firms have voluntarily introduced some form of worker representation, mostly a works council, elected by the enterprise workforce. There is not much national uniformity, however.

Both the highly institutionalized Austrian system of labor relations and the flexible and decentralized Swiss system are the subject of discussion about (still) more flexibility. Both systems have been highly stable, however, and even the compulsory membership of the employee and employer chambers in Austria is not a bone of contention.

PORTUGAL AND SPAIN

Even more than Belgium and Holland, Portugal and Spain have been large colonial powers. They were late in industrializing compared to the rest of Western Europe, which gave rise to a large emigration of labor, in particular to France. In terms of population size Portugal, with 10.5 million inhabitants, is a small country, while Spain, with almost 40 million inhabitants, is more of a mid-sized nation--ranking between the small nations with up to 15 million inhabitants and the large countries with over 55 million people.

Although both still lag behind the rest of Western Europe in industrial development, industry has overtaken agriculture as the major source of employment since the 1960s. Industry is still heavily concentrated in a few old industrial regions--like the large cities in Portugal, and Catalonia, the Basque country and Asturias in northern Spain. Both countries are now following in the footsteps of Western Europe by becoming service-oriented economies. National politics have long been a battlefield between conservative and rural Catholic ("clerical") interests, on the one hand and anti-clerical liberals and socialists in the cities and the industrial centers on the other. Both countries also had a sizable anarchist labor movement in the first decades of the twentieth century. Together with the communists and socialists it was smashed by fascist dictatorships, which were established in the 1930s--in Spain after the bloody Civil War. While Spanish fascism paid only lip service to state corporatism, Portugal became a major exponent of this kind of authoritarian corporatism. State-controlled unions negotiated with employers, but even the process of bargaining was heavily monitored by the state. Since the end of fascist rule in the 1970s both countries have become democracies, in which the trade unions form the core of the political opposition to the national governments. The two countries differ in the nature of these government-union relations.

In Portugal a radical socialist revolution in 1974 succeeded fascism. Although it was short-lived, one of its landmarks, the nationalization of large enterprise, still stands. The privatization of this sector is one of the issues in the union opposition to the conservative parties that dominate Portuguese politics. The largest trade union movement is a communist one, still hailing the record of the 1974 revolution and trying to defend its accomplisments. Its stronghold is in the nationalized shipyards and public transport. The socialist union movement, more moderate in its aims, is much smaller. The size of the nationalized sector, including major industries, has also served to maintain a high level of union militancy and union density (at least for Latin standards), of almost thirty percent. Spain has undergone an easier transition from fascism to democracy, and a highly reformist socialist party has been in power since the early 1980s. Union opposition to the socialist governments has been less steady and less unified, due to the existence of a large socialist union confederation. In the late 1970s, right after the end of fascism, the communist-dominated union movement was the largest one, as in Portugal. Communists had established strong oppositional networks in industry and were able to build their organizations on the basis of these illegal committees. The Spanish communist-dominated union confederation is still named after these workers' committees (*comisiones obreras*). In Spain the socialist movement--to some extent linked to the socialist party--was able to overtake the communist-dominated one, however, due in part to all kinds of formal and informal government support. That support did not keep this movement from time to time joining political protest against state measures, however. Trade union membership has dropped rapidly since the early 1980s to less than twenty percent currently.

As in France, permanent organization of union members is less important than sporadic or more frequent mobilization for strikes, including political actions in which the public sector and public transport play a major role. The actions are hampered by ideological discord between the confederations and even more by ideological diversity within the confederations and by their reliance on scattered local strongholds. As in the other Latin countries, notions like "communist-dominated" actually mean dominated by radical locals, which are close to the communist party but with strong anarchist, radical socialist and even radical Christian currents. The actions are also hampered by the governments' insistence on the need to adapt to Western European standards--and especially in Spain by the high unemployment of almost twenty percent, the highest rate in Europe.

Although Spanish legislation regarding worker participation has adopted some German features, in both countries the union representation monopolizes worker participation. The works council elections are even called trade union elections in Spain. The distinction between bargaining issues and worker participation topics is hardly made, and the local unions are heavily involved in both, as well as in organizing strikes.

The national governments have been the driving force behind efforts at tripartism and the establishment of tripartite councils. The main obstacles to a development in that direction have been employer resistance and trade union division. Portugal set up a tripartite council in 1984, and in Spain the discussion on the use of such a body lingered on for almost a decade. More important than these new institutions (which, like their French and Italian counterparts, are too large and include too many interests to be effective) have been tripartite agreements, mainly on wage restraint and even incidental nationwide bargaining, between the peak organizations. Both the employers' confederations and the communist-dominated unions are reluctant to participate in such talks, and on several occasions they have refused to sign the agreement. A new wave of optimism about cooperative labor relations follows each agreement, but the unions point to the nationwide strikes, in particular against revision of the fascist legislation on dismissals, rather than to the agreements as major contributions to national politics and labor relations. A new "mediation pact" concluded by the Spanish confederations in January 1996 aimed at a change in this culture of conflict. It introduced mediation procedures and established a joint mediation service, without direct government involvement.

HUNGARY AND POLAND

The difference in population size between Hungary (10.7 million inhabitants) and Poland (38.6 million) is comparable to that between Portugal and Spain. Both countries were late industrializers compared to most of Western Europe. As in most of Latin Europe industry was limited to a few industrial regions, like the national capital in Hungary and the central and southwestern parts of Poland like Silezia. Until World War II the social democratic labor movement outnumbered the communist (and in Poland also the Catholic) unions, but periods of large regional labor revolts alternated with times in which trade unionism was suppressed. World War II especially affected Poland, which lost a sizable part of its population and was completely devastated. After World War II both countries came under communist control and became part of the Soviet Russia-dominated Communist Bloc. Since the demise of Russian communism Hungary and Poland have been engaged in a transition towards parliamentary democracy and private enterprise. While Poland is still in large part an industrial country (over one third of its labor force is employed in industry), the majority of Hungarian workers are employed in services. Both countries suffer from a high unemployment rate of over fifteen percent and Poland also from running inflation.

In neither country did the 1989 overthrow come all of a sudden. After Russian troops smashed a national revolt in 1956, Hungary slowly became the most liberal economy of the communist bloc, in which there was some scope for private enterprise--and in the 1980s also for rather autonomous trade unions. The country developed a relatively large private sector outside the reach of the communist party. The communists lost part of their control over the economy, but they retained their power monopoly in politics. In Poland this monopoly was challenged in 1980 by the rise of Solidarność. It started as a strike committee in the shipyards of Gdańsk, but soon extended its scope and its range of demands beyond questions of wages and prices. It subsequently grew to a membership of nine million, second only to the TUC in Europe, and for over a year it competed for political power with the communist party. Under pressure of Russian intervention the party dictatorship suppressed Solidarność at the end of 1981, without putting its leader Lech Walesa on trial. At the end of the 1980s Solidarność was again legalized--to become a major political movement and to see its leader elected as president of the country in the first free elections after communism.

The difference between early economic reform in Hungary and trade unionism as a massive political movement in Poland still has an impact on the nature of trade unionism and employers' organizations. The Hungarian trade union movement, with a tradition of apolitical muddling-through in the expanding private sector, is highly fragmented. It consists of six new confederations, established since 1989, and the former communist organization, which outnumbers the other six put together. The employers' side is equally divided, with at least four organizations claiming to represent private enterprise in industry. In Poland the union scene is still dominated by Solidarność, which has been unable to grow to its formidable 1980 membership numbers and the (by now larger) former communist union confederation. One employer confederation represents all private enterprise. A major source of friction between the trade unions has been the allocation of the assets of the communist unions, claimed by the heir organizations. The issue has been solved in Hungary after fierce inter-union struggle. A second source of friction is the one between workers in the public enterprises, bearing the burden of the economic transformation, and the workers in the growing private economy.

Solidarność has been a major political actor in Poland during and after the nation's political transition. Not only did it actively promote the establishment of employers' organizations, it has also acted as a political party, participating in elections. Its alleged moderation has occasioned the rise of a more radical split-off called Solidarność '80. Moreover, the Polish confederations have also been active in politics by calling or supporting strikes against economic policy and labor conditions in the state sector, which still employs over forty percent of all workers, far more than in Hungary. This state sector enhances the importance of the national government in labor relations, in addition to its role in the framing of new laws regulating relations between employers and unions and employees. Major examples of this legislation are the Hungarian 1989 Strike Act and 1992 Labor Code, the Polish Acts on Trade Unions and Employers' Organizations and on Collective Dispute Settlement--both dating from 1991--as well as the 1994 Act on Collective Bargaining.

At first Solidarność refused to engage in any form of tripartism. That decision was motivated by its influence as a political movement and the weakness of the emerging employers' associations. It was not until 1993 that a tripartite pact provided for a National Tripartite Committee for Social and Economic Problems. The Hungarian unions were too divided and lacked the historic predisposition for such a preponderant role in national politics. They cooperated in efforts to establish a tripartite body. A precursor to this National Reconciliation Council (*Érdekegyeztető Tanács*, ÉT) was already established in 1988, right before the turn towards democracy. The Council has been active in the deregulation of wage determination and in conflict settlement. Its major accomplishment in the latter area was the resolution of the 1990 three-day taxi drivers blockade in the capital Budapest after a rise in fuel prices. The unions' attitude during that conflict points to a distinction between political and industrial union activities which is hardly matched in Poland.

In both countries the union confederations, as well as their member organizations, are still loose structures, only to some extent coordinating the union representation or works councils within the enterprise. This enterprise or even shop floor level is the main level of collective bargaining currently, within limits posed by the national government--in Hungary after consultation with the tripartite council. The councils have a longer tradition in Poland, where they emerged spontaneously in the mid-1950s. In 1980 Solidarność revived the councils, and after their legal regulation they continued to exist under communist control. Since the collapse of communism they are dominated by the post-communist trade union organization. In Hungary nationwide council elections have been held since 1992, when the post-communist unions gained over forty percent of the seats, more than twice as much as the second largest organization. In both countries a distinction is made between the works councils and the trade union representation, which takes care of collective bargaining. Branch bargaining is almost nonexistent in both countries, due to the weakness of employers' organizations and the unions themselves.

11

A Summary in American Terms

This summary applies a number of American labor relations terms to European labor relations in order to show more clearly the specific nature of the latter. Its purpose is not a comparison. For that reason, the references to labor relations in the United States are very short.

LABOR RELATIONS AND POLITICS

European and U.S. labor relations share a few common features, including the political involvement of trade unions and employers, the development of a body of basic laws regulating labor relations in the course of the twentieth century and the current trend towards decentralization. Even on the few common points Europe and the US show great differences, however. The differences are expressed in everyday language and in labor relations terminology. Common American terms--ranging from agency shop, business unionism and certification to whipsawing and whistle blowing--are hardly used in Europe. The major exception is Great Britain, which shares a number of common features with U.S. labor relations. Since the rest of this chapter underscores the differences between labor relations in the United States and in Europe, from now on "Europe" will stand for Continental Western Europe--that is, for the Latin and Germanic countries, without the British Isles.

Probably the core distinguishing feature of European labor relations is the strong link in Europe between the industrial or economic arena--in which unions, employers and employers' associations operate--and the political arena. This link was forged, especially by the labor movement, at the end of the nineteenth century. In the United States the combination of industrial and political activities has been introduced on a few occasions, but it failed. Several explanations have been forwarded for this "American exceptionalism." Applied to Europe, an economic explanation would be that at the end of the nineteenth century the labor market was less tight in Europe than in the United States, which negatively affected the position of skilled workers. These workers then turned to politics, to become the backbone of the socialist parties that sprang up and also tried to recruit the less skilled workers for their political action. A social explanation refers to the nature of social and cultural division. In most of Europe only religious cleavages hampered the rise of a general labor movement appealing to all workers, while division along lines of nationality did not. Moreover, this religious split was activated by Catholics only and mainly played a role in countries with a mixed Protestant and Catholic population. In the predominantly Catholic nations--that is in Latin Europe--the early secularization of the working class was one of the reasons that Catholic efforts to set up their own labor organizations were less effective.

A point often stressed in the United States and in Great Britain is the legal tradition of the European Continent. Since the French Revolution most of Europe has adopted a tradition of civil law, established by legislation, which only leaves small margins for court rulings. In contrast, the Anglo-Saxon tradition of common law leaves ample latitude for judges to establish rules by precedent. European rulers and parliaments would not have left to the courts the decision that workers' associations were lawful (as in the U.S. case of Commonwealth v. Hunt, 1842) or the application of anti-trust legislation (as in the U.S. 1890 Sherman Anti-Trust Act). If courts were to apply such laws, parliaments and governments would change the law if they disapproved of the interpretation by judges. Since this difference points to the position of the national parliaments, the distinctive feature is not one of legal tradition but a political one in the timing of democratization. During the nineteenth century all Continental countries had a less democratic political system than did the United States (for its Caucasian population). Voting rights were limited and, in contrast to the United States, the early political parties only appealed to the feudal class, industrialists and the upper middle class. This made the labor movement create its own parties. Second, the early workers' movement in Europe was not fighting against conservative applications of democratic constitutions, but against dictatorial of quasi-dictatorial rulers or governments and against parliaments that had been elected under conditions of very limited suffrage rights. These conservative institutions constituted better targets for political struggle by national labor movements than the diverse court rulings in the United States.

It was not only labor's drive, legal traditions and the nature of European politics that stimulated the link between the economic and the political arena. The two world wars (1914-18 and 1939-45) constituted additional impetus, in combination with the fact that the labor movement had developed as a major political force. The war efforts and wartime suffering urged some form of labor integration into national politics. Large postwar strikes after both wars and the need for economic recovery reinforced that trend. Calling the U.S. New Deal labor legislation "late" actually implies that wars are considered normal facts of European politics--since they hastened social developments in Europe and gave it the lead in social policies. The strike wave after World War II was silenced by labor's participation in the national government, including the communists in France and Italy--a different outcome from that of the 1947 Taft-Hartley Act in the United States. Because the choice for labor integration in Europe had already been made at the end of World War I, the Taft-Hartley Act, or anything like it, did not fit into European politics and labor relations by the end of World War II.

However, large parts of Europe had also fallen victim to a conservative reaction to the rise of labor to power between the wars. It had taken the form of outright suppression of the labor movement and forced integration of the working class into a fascist political system. Indeed, more than the United States, Europe alternated between political integration and suppression of the labor movement in the first half of the twentieth century, with a definite turn towards integration at the end of World War II. The integration of labor, in particular in Germanic Europe, and its important and recognized oppositional role in Latin Europe, prevented corruption and links with organized crime--or at least reduced these social and political evils to a level accepted in national politics and the national economy at large. Hence, the 1959 Landrum Griffin Act would not have fit the European pattern of postwar integration either. Moreover, any piece of legislation on internal democracy would also have applied to other social and political organizations, including the employers' associations, and in most European countries the latter were more known for their secrecy than the trade unions. Singling out the unions for specific restrictive legislation would have been unthinkable after World War II, due to the political strength and the integration of labor.

The politicization of the labor movement in the late nineteenth century encouraged the transition from craft unions to industrial unionism, in contrast to the rivalry between the AFL's craft unions and CIO's industrial unions in the US. Labor's politicization and the close link between the industrial and the political arena, as well as the expansion of the national governments at the end of the wars, had yet another effect on the labor movement and employers' associations--the growing importance or even dominance of the national confederations. Only in Germany was this confederate power reduced after World War II, partly under American and British pressure. Without exception, the national confederations were officially recognized as the national representatives of labor right after World War II. This recognition was either confirmed by law or remained a matter of informal political understanding, without much difference for labor relations practice. In this respect there exists no differentiation between friends and foes. Confederations taking part in corporatist talks are recognized, as are confederations whose main aim is to overthrow the national government.

EMPLOYER-UNION CONTACTS

European sector bargaining is more than "multi-employer bargaining." The difference with single-employer negotiations is not only the number of employers involved but also the predominance of sector or branch organizations on both sides. Although the employers' bargaining delegations may include prominent employers, it is the employers' organizations as such that engage in the talks, assume responsibility for the outcome, submit the results to their members for approval--and in exceptional cases expel dissenting or non-compliant employers. On the union side, member organizations of the national confederations take part in sector as well as in enterprise bargaining. Their activities are not conditional to any form of certification or union election, other than national recognition of the union confederations. Independent sector unions may also try to take part in the negotiations, but their participation is subject to approval of the member organizations of the recognized confederations. The decision to admit such independent organizations is based upon their membership and strike potential-- that is, it is a matter of force, not of election. Hence the importance of the recent debate in some countries to recognize new confederations and allow them to join corporatist talks. That recognition will automatically put an end to any exclusion of their members, whatever their size, in sector negotiations.

The predominance of sector bargaining implies that the economic sector or industrial branch is the normal "bargaining unit" in Europe. The only other bargaining units are the country as a whole, in case of all-industry bargaining, and the company (or the plant) as the smallest unit, although plant negotiations are uncommon. At any bargaining level all workers are covered, with only two exceptions. First, in a number of countries there are separate agreements for manual and clerical workers, both at the sector and enterprise level. The second exception is higher echelon workers, who have their own collective agreements, or are not covered by collective bargaining. Sector bargaining also means that the notion of an "exclusive bargaining agent" does not exist. If there is only one national union confederation, its sector union is automatically the only bargaining partner of the employers. If there are more confederations, all their sector organizations may take part.

New rounds of sector negotiations mostly start in the same branch each year. In particular the well-unionized machine construction industries, including car manufacture, act as pioneers in the European way of "pattern bargaining." The other sectors adopt the outcome in those branches as a yardstick for their own negotiations. Only exceptionally will other well-unionized industries, like printing, take over as pacesetters. This more or less fixed form of pattern bargaining does not leave much latitude for whipsawing. In practice, there is a lot of regional and local whipsawing in case of enterprise negotiations, but this is a marginal phenomenon because of the impact of sector bargaining. The main example of union efforts to shift bargaining to a sector that seems more promising has been between the public sector and the private sector. The national governments have been just as eager, however, to use the public sector as an example of wage restraint.

Due to the widespread tradition of sector bargaining, the distinction between "union companies" and "non-union companies" does not make much sense in most European countries. Companies do not have to bargain, since in most cases they will be covered by sector agreements. The notion of "non-union firm" would apply almost exclusively to large companies that are covered by enterprise agreements only and refuse to bargain for a new agreement. This is mainly a Latin European phenomenon but often the non-union period does not last very long and the company will resume at least some form of formal contact with the unions after a few years of cold war. In several countries the main union instrument against such an unwilling employer is to ask for the legal extension of the sector agreements. That would force the company to adopt the sector labor conditions. (Of course, that strategy does not work if the company normally pays more than the sector average, which is often the case in large enterprises.) The larger scale of bargaining also leads to larger and fewer labor conflicts than in the United States, to less "picketing" and to fewer individual or collective "walkouts." Strikes in Latin Europe can be very short and show some similarity with American walkouts, but employees in Germanic Europe only walk out when the working day is over. When the continental unions call a strike, they often fix the date in advance, and they are bound by legal and other obligations to follow procedures of conflict and conflict resolution. They do not ask the general public to support the action--for instance, by a "boycott"--since that would turn it into a conflict with that particular employer rather than with the sector employers' organization. The European boycott slogan would have to be "Don't buy a car, any car," rather than "Don't buy a Ford," or "Don't call anyone" instead of "Boycot AT&T."

This overview shows that in Europe, and in the Germanic nations most of all, it is the activities of organizations that count in labor relations, not individual actions by workers--or even by employers. Individual workers have more or less given up the right of initiative in favor of protection, which in their eyes is what the unions are for. Indeed, the unions leave less initiative with workers and offer more protection in return than do the unions in the United States, where any worker action may lead to a counterattack by the employer.

The European situation might be summarized as one in which the unions will bargain for any worker, whether he or she is willing to join them or not. The only alternative for employees is to start a new sector union, which is not an easy task. Europe lacks the enterprise-based union elections, which may be more democratic in principle but leave ample room for employer efforts to influence them. One of the effects of this difference is that Europe lacks the American abundance of labor lawyers who make a living out of fighting the unions. Instead, that money is spent (though not always wholeheartedly) on company departments that deal with worker participation. The difference is also expressed in the academic interest. European books on labor relations, like this one, mainly focus on the interplay between organizations and the national government--in other words, on relations outside the enterprise rather than on relations within the enterprise.

WORKER PARTICIPATION

In European countries where labor relations are "adversarial," the term often used for U.S. labor relations, this cold war nature of labor relations is mitigated by the shift of union-employer relations from within to outside the enterprise. The center of gravity in European labor relations is outside the enterprise--in sector and branch activities, in national bargaining and corporatism and in national politics.

The shift to sector and all-industry activities affects the feasibility of "company unions." Such unions existed until World War I, and some even survived that war. However, they have had harder times in Europe than in the United States, since they are excluded from the main employer-union contacts. In addition, they have met with overt hostility from the national government and even from employers' associations, because they undermine the representational monopoly of the major union confederation as well as the major employers' confederations --and hence also affect the impact of sector and national bargaining. Because of this general hostility, company unions are a highly marginal phenomenon in European labor relations. Not only the company union, but also the company involved is more or less treated as an outlaw.

Since World War II the European unions have developed a new foothold within the enterprise in the form of worker participation by works councils or the trade union representation. This feature of European labor relations has brought the unions back in, as a kind of opposition force within the enterprise. Because their priority is with the activities at higher levels, the unions have had to act as a "loyal opposition," committing their members to productivity growth, which serves as a major base of wage determination in sector bargaining. Thus, employers and unions, as well as works councils, share a common commitment to labor peace and enterprise productivity. It is in worker participation that union elections play a role, since they decide about the relative union strength within the worker participation institutions. In a few nations and sectors with a low union density the non-union members are currently gaining more and more seats in such institutions. However, even in the highly fictional case of a complete non-union monopoly of works councils, the enterprise would still not be a "non-union" one in the American (and British) sense, since it would remain subject to sector agreements.

Related to the primacy of sector bargaining and to trade union pluralism is the relative absence of the "closed shop" or the "union shop" in Europe. Unions have preferred a strong sector base rather than a monopoly position in specific enterprises. In practice the high union density in the traditional strongholds of trade unionism sometimes lead to a "hidden" form of closed shop, but the union position has never been strong enough to enforce a completely closed shop or union shop. Even if the unions had been able to do so, they would have been stopped by legislation, supported by the social democrats, which forbids any discrimination as to union membership. As a consequence, "right-to-work legislation" in the American (and British) sense does not exist either. In Europe right-to-work legislation would either refer to measures to reduce unemployment or to employee protection against arbitrary dismissal, not to measures directed against trade union power. The only instance of right-to-work protection of employees against the unions would occur if a trade union dismissed its own employees and the latter appealed to a court. This is a rare event, and if it happens it always gets a wide coverage in the national mass media ("Latest news: Unions dismiss workers!").

In most European countries a discussion on employer financial support of enterprise-based union activities, as exemplified in the 1994 Dunlop report in the United States, is not very relevant. Most employers are under the legal (or other) obligation to provide ample funds for worker participation activities and sometimes also for specific union tasks, like training works council members. This is not to say that recent developments such as quality groups and human resoures management may not be a threat to the union role within the enterprise. Indeed, they are, due to the fact that they promote a view of the unions as "outside intruders." The unions are meeting the new challenges, however, by developing new tasks and functions as a loyal opposition movement, in order to avoid the "Americanization" of labor relations.

THE EUROPEAN WELFARE STATE

The integration of European labor in national politics has contributed to the rise and the stability of the European welfare state. In contrast to its function in the United States, "welfare" does not refer to a system of allowances that mainly benefit specific groups of the population, like unmarried black mothers. Rather, it denotes "prosperity" and welfare state refers to a society in which this prosperity has reached high standards for most of the population, because of the combination of high wages and relatively high benefits from national income maintenance policies. These policies do make some differentiation between benefits for those who paid contributions and those who did not, but the strict separation between earned social security and unearned welfare that exists in the United States, hardly applies in Europe. The European version of the "American Dream," serving as a source of inspiration for individual careers towards wealth and power, is a "European nightmare," showing all kinds of political, social, economic and personal evils which may lead to a loss of income. The nightmare encourages collective provisions to compensate for that loss. In other words, Europeans are more concerned with what happens in case the "American Dream" does not come true. Extensive legal sanctioning of basic labor conditions forms a part of that protection. Recent cuts in welfare spending have affected the level of social security benefits, but they have not shaken the basic idea of the welfare state.

The integration of labor at the national level culminates in the corporatism of the smaller states. This term has the same Latin root as the word "corporation" or "corporate," but the European term refers to any organizational body of people--including trade unions--rather than just to companies. Corporatism and tripartism allow for a kind of national solidarity in wage bargaining, including wage concessions by the union confederations. Indeed, national and sector bargaining is a permanent combination of "normal" and "concessionary" bargaining, depending upon economic and political conditions. Paradoxically, this national solidarity has not only contributed to high wages but also to long holidays of four to six weeks, often with double pay for at least part of that period. The extension of holidays is due to the fact that the European unions have demanded such a reduction in work time both in periods of a tight labor market, in order to alleviate the work-load, and in periods of unemployment, in order to better allocate the available amount of work.

In combination with cooperative worker participation national and sector bargaining in the Germanic countries has made the Germanic unions more business-minded that their U.S. counterparts. They are not "business unions" in the American sense since they form part of a wider political movement and promote societal change, but in practice they have come to promote national business and enterprise productivity in addition to wage increases.

As a consequence, there are hardly any "non-union states" in Europe--that is, countries in which labor interests are not taken into account and trade unionism is not supported in one way or another. Any investment shift that is going on in Europe is one from high-wage to low-wage countries rather than one from "union states" to "non-union states." Some American features are creeping in, however, in both Latin and Germanic Europe. These include the crisis of nationwide bargaining, the reduced role of the unions in national politics, the decentralization of bargaining to the enterprise and the spread of low-pay and low-security jobs as part of a wider development towards enterprise and labor market flexibility. However, even for many European employers a total "Americanization" of labor relations is still more of a frightening idea than an ideal.

Bibliography

* The bibliography listings marked with an asterisk consist only or mainly of nation surveys.

Adams, Roy J. (1995). *Industrial Relations under Liberal Democracy: North America in Comparative Perspective*. Columbia SC: University of South Carolina Press.

Baglioni, Guido, and Colin Crouch, eds. (1990). *European Industrial Relations: The Challenge of Flexibility*. London: Sage.*

Baldwin-Edwards, Martin, and Martin A. Schain, eds. (1994). "The Politics of Immigration in Western Europe." *West European Politics*, Special Issue, vol. 17, no. 2.

Bamber, Greg B., and Russell D. Lansbury, eds. (1993). *International and Comparative Industrial Relations*. London: Routledge.*

Barnouin, Barbara (1986). *The European Labour Movement and European Integration*. London: Frances Pinter.

Bean, Ron, and Ken Holden (1992). "Cross-national Differences in Trade Union Membership in OECD Countries." *Industrial Relations Journal*, vol. 23, 52-59

Bercusson, Brian (1993). European Labour Law and Sectoral Bargaining." *Industrial Relations Review*, vol. 24, 257-272.

Blanpain, R., ed. (1987). *Comparative Labour Law and Industrial Relations*. Deventer: Kluwer.

Brunetta, Renato, and Carlo Dell'Aringa, eds. (1990). *Labour Relations and*

Economic Performance. London: Macmillan.

Calmfors, Lars, ed. (1990). *Wage Formation and Macro-Economic Policy in the Nordic Countries*. Oxford: Oxford University Press.

Cameron, David (1984). "Social Democracy, Corporatism, Labour Quiescence and the Representation of Economic Interest in Advanced Capitalist Society." In John P. Goldthorpe, ed., *Order and Conflict in Contemporary Capitalism*. Oxford: Clarendon Press, 143-178.

Carley, Mark (1993). "Social Dialogue." In: Michael Gold, ed., *The Social Dimension: Employment Policy in the European Community*. Basingstoke: Macmillan, 105-134.

Castles, Francis G. (1987a). *The Impact of Parties: Politics and Policies in Democratic Capitalist States*. London: Sage.

- - - (1987b). "Neocorporatism and the 'Happiness Index', or What the Trade Unions Get for Their Cooperation." *European Journal of Political Research*, vol. 15, 381-393.

- - - (1994). "On Religion and Public Policy: Does Catholicism Make a Difference?" *European Journal of Political Research*, vol. 25, 19-40.

Castles, Francis G., Franz Lehner, and Manfred G. Schmidt, eds. (1988). *Managing Mixed Economies*. Berlin: Walter de Gruyter.

Clegg, Hugh (1976). *Trade Unionism under Collective Bargaining: A Theory Based on Comparisons of Six Countries*. Oxford: Basil Blackwell.

Compston, Hugh (1994). "Union Participation in Economic Policy-Making in Austria, Switzerland, The Netherlands, Belgium and Ireland, 1970-1992." *West European Politics*, vol. 17 no. 1, 123-145.

Corbey, Dorette (1995). "Dialectical Functionalism: Stagnation as a Booster to Integration." *International Organization*, vol. 49 no. 2, 253-284.

Cox, Andrew, and Noel O'Sullivan, eds. (1988). *The Corporate State: Corporatism and the State Tradition in Western Europe*. Aldershot: Edward Elgar.

Cox, Susan (1993). "Equal Opportunities." In Michael Gold, ed., *The Social Dimension: Employment Policy in the European Community*. Basingstoke: Macmillan, 41-63.

Cressey, Peter, and Robin Williams (1990). *Participation in Change: New Technology and the Role of Employee Involvement*. Dublin: European Foundation for the Improvement of Living and Working Conditions.

Crouch, Colin (1993). *Industrial Relations and European State Traditions*. Oxford: Clarendon Press.

- - - (1994). "Beyond Corporatism: The Impact of Company Strategy." In Richard Hyman, and Anthony Ferner, eds. , *New Frontiers in European Industrial Relations*. Oxford: Basil Blackwell, 196-222.

Crouch, Colin, and A. Pizzorno, eds. (1978). *The Resurgence of Class Conflict in Western Europe since 1968* (2 vols). New York: Homes and Meier.

De Swaan, Abram (1988). *In Care of the State: Health Care, Education and Welfare in Europe and the USA in the Modern Era*. Cambridge: Polity Press.

Dell'Aringa, Carlo, and Manuela Samek Lodovici (1992). "Industrial Relations and Economic Performance." In Tiziano Treu, ed., *Participation in Public Policy-Making: The Role of Trade Unions and Employers' Associations*. Berlin: Walter de Gruyter, 26-58.

Delsen, Lei (1995). *Atypical Employment: An International Perspective*. Groningen: Wolters-Noordhof.

Due, Jesper, Jörgen Steen Madsen, and Carsten Strøby Jensen (1991). "The Social Dimension: Convergence or Diversification of Industrial Relations in the Single European Market." *Industrial Relations Journal*, vol. 22, 85-102.

Edwards, Richard, Paolo Garonna, and Franz Toedtling, eds. (1986). *Union in Crisis and Beyond: Perspectives from Six Countries*. Dover, MA: Auburn House.

Esping-Andersen, Gösta (1990). *The Three Worlds of Welfare Capitalism*. Princeton NJ: Princeton University Press.

Esping-Andersen, Gösta, and Walter Korpi (1984). "Social Policy as Class Politics in Post-War Capitalism: Scandinavia, Austria and Germany." In J. Goldthorpe, ed., *Order and Conflict in Contemporary Capitalism*. Oxford: Clarendon Press, 179-208.

Ferner, Anthony (1994). "The State as Employer." In Richard Hyman and
        Anthony Ferner, eds., *New Frontiers in European Industrial Relations*.
        Oxford: Basil Blackwell, 52-79.

Ferner, Anthony and Richard Hyman, eds. (1992). *Industrial Relations in the
        New Europe*. Oxford: Basil Blackwell.*

Flanagan, Robert J., David W. Soskice, and Lloyd Ulman (1983). *Unionism,
        Economic Stabilization and Income Policies: European Experience*.
        Washington: The Brookings Institution.*

Flora, Peter, ed. (1986). *Growth to Limits: The Western European Welfare
        States since World War II*. Berlin: Walter de Gruyter.

Flora, Peter, and Jens Alber (1981). "Modernization, Democratization and the
        Development of Welfare States in Europe." In Peter Flora and Arnold
        Heidenheimer, eds., *The Development of Welfare States in Europe and
        America*. London: Transaction Books.

Geary, Dick (1981). *European Labour Protest 1848-1939*. London: Croom
        Helm.

Geul, Arend, Paul Nobelen, and Hans Slomp (1986). "The Future of
        Tripartism in the Low Countries." In Mark D. Ten Hove, ed., *The
        Institutions of a Changing Welfare State*. Maastricht: Presses
        interuniversitaires européennes, 17-34.

Gill, Colin (1993). "Technological Change and Participation in Work
        Organization: Recent Results from a European Community Survey.
        International Journal of Human Resource Management, vol. 4, 325-348.

Gill, Colin, and Hubert Krieger (1992). "The Diffusion of Participation in
        New Information Technology in Europe: Survey Results." *Economic and
        industrial Democracy*, vol. 13, 331-358.

Gladstone, Alan ed. (1989). *Current Issues in Labour Relations: An
        International Perspective*. Berlin: Walter de Gruyter.

Gold, Michael ed., (1993). *The Social Dimension: Employment Policy in the
        European Community*. Basingstoke: Macmillan.

Gold, Michael, and Mark Hall (1992). *Report on European-level Information
        and Consultation in Multinational Companies: An Evaluation of
        Practice*. Dublin: European Foundation for the Improvement of Living

and Working Conditions.

Golden, Miriam, and Jonas Pontusson, eds. (1992). *Bargaining for Change: Union Politics in North America and Europe*. Ithaca NY: Cornell University Press.

Goldthorpe, John P., ed. (1984). *Order and Conflict in Contemporary Capitalism*. Oxford: Clarendon Press.

Gourevitch, Peter, (1984). *Unions and Economic Crisis: Britain, West Germany, and Sweden*. London: George Allen and Unwin.*

Grahl, John, and Paul Teague (1989). "Labour Market Flexibility in West Germany, Britain and France." *West European Politics*, vol. 12, no. 2, 91-111.

Greenwood, Justin, Juergen R. Grote, and Karsten Ronit, eds. (1992). *Organized Interests and the European Community*. London: Sage.

Hall, Mark (1994). "Industrial Relations and the Social Dimension of European Integration: Before and After Maastricht." In Richard Hyman and Anthony Ferner, eds., *New Frontiers in European Industrial Relations*. Oxford: Basil Blackwell, 281-311.

Hancké, Bob (1993). "Trade Union Membership in Europe 1960-1990: Rediscovering Local Unions. British *Journal of Industrial Relations*, vol. 31, 592-613.

Hancké, Bob, and Hans Slomp (1996). "A Small Difference with Large Consequences: Local and National Unions in Postwar Belgium and The Netherlands." In Richard M. Locke and Kathleen Thelen, eds., *The Shifting Boundaries of Labor Politics: New Directions for Comparative Research and Theory*. Cambridge MA: M.I.T. Press (forthcoming).

Hartley, Jean F. (1992). "Joining a Trade Union." In Jean F. Hartley and Geoffrey M. Stephenson, eds., *Employment Relations*. Oxford: Basil Blackwell, 163-183.

Harzing, Anne-Wil, and Joris Van Ruysseveldt, eds. (1995). *International Human Resource Management: An Integrated Approach*. London: Sage.

HBS (1992). *Japanization, or going our own way? Internalization and Interest Representation*. Düsseldorf: Hans Böckler Stiftung.

Henly, Andrew, and Euclid Tsakalotos (1992). "Corporatism and the
     European Labour Market after 1992." *British Journal of Industrial
     Relations*, vol. 30, 567-586

Héthy, Lajos (1994). "Tripartism in Eastern Europe." In Richard Hyman and
     Anthony Ferner, eds., *New Frontiers in European Industrial Relations*.
     Oxford: Basil Blackwell, 312-336.

Howell, Chris (1992). *Regulating Labor: The State and Industrial Relations
     Reform in Postwar France*. Princeton NJ: Princeton University Press.

Hyman, Richard, and Wolfgang Streeck, eds. (1988). *New Technology and
     Industrial Relations*. Oxford: Basil Blackwell.

IDE (1993). *Industrial Democracy in Europe Revisited*. Oxford: Oxford
     University Press.

James, Phil (1993). "Occupational Health and Safety." In Michael Gold, ed.,
     The Social Dimension: Employment Policy in the European Community.
     Basingstoke: Macmillan, 135-172.

Katz, Harry C. (1993). "The Decentralization of Collective Bargaining: A
     Literature Review and Comparative Analysis." *Industrial and Labor
     Relations Review*, vol. 47, 3-22.

Katzenstein, Peter J. (1984). *Corporatism and Change: Austria, Switzerland
     and the Politics of Industry*. Ithaca NY: Cornell University Press.

- - - (1985). *Small States in World Markets: Industrial Policy in Europe*.
     Ithaca NY: Cornell University Press.

Katznelson, Ira, and Aristide Zolberg, eds. (1986). *Working Class
     Formation: Nineteenth-Century Patterns in Western Europe and the
     United States*. Princeton NJ: Princeton University Press.

Koelble, Thomas A. (1988). "Challenges to the Trade Unions: The British
     and West German Cases." *West European Politics*, vol. 11, no. 3, 92-
     109.

Korpi, Walter (1983). *The Democratic Class Struggle*. London: Routledge
     and Kegan Paul.

Korpi, Walter, and Michael Shalev (1979). "Strikes, Industrial Relations and
     Class conflict in Capitalist Societies." *British Journal of Sociology*, vol.

Bibliography   155

30, 215-239

Kurzer, Paulette (1991). "The Internationalization of Business and Domestic Class Compromises: A Four Country Study." *West European Politics*, vol. 14 no. 4, 1-24.

Lane, Christel (1989). *Management and Labour in Europe*. Aldershot: Edward Elgar.

Lange, Peter (1984). "Unions, Workers, and Wage Regulation: The Rational Bases of Consent." In John P. Goldthorpe, ed., *Order and Conflict in Contemporary Capitalism*. Oxford: Clarendon Press, 98-123.

- - - (1993). "Maastricht and the Social Protocol: Why did They Do It?" *Politics and Society*, vol. 21, 5-36

Lange, Peter, George Ross, and Maurizio Vannicelli (1982). *Unions, Change and Crisis: French and Italian Union Strategy and the Political Economy, 1945-1980*. London: George Allen and Unwin.*

Lehmbruch, Gerhard (1977). "Liberal Corporatism and Party Government." *Comparative Political Studies*, vol. 10, 91-127.

Lehmbruch, Gerhard, and Philippe C. Schmitter, eds. (1982). *Patterns of Corporatist Policy Making*. London: Sage.

Lewin, David, Olivia S. Mitchell, and Peter D. Sherer, eds. (1992). *Research Frontiers in Industrial Relations and Human Resources*. Madison, WI: Industrial Relations Research Institute.

Locke, Richard M. (1990). "The Resurgence of the Local Union: Restructuring and Industrial Relations in Italy." *Politics and Society*, vol. 18, 229-249.

- - - (1992). "The Demise of the National Union in Italy: Lessons for Comparative Industrial Relations Theory." *Industrial and Labor Relations Review*, Vol. 45, 229-249.

Luebbert, Gregory M. (1991). *Liberalism, Fascism, or Social Democracy: Social Classes and the political Origins of Regimes in Interwar Europe*. Oxford: Oxford University Press.

Maier, Charles S. (1975). *Recasting Bourgeois Europe: Stabilization in France, Germany, and Italy in the Decade after World War I*. Princeton

NJ: Princeton University Press.

Marginson, Paul, Arend Buitendam, Christoph Deutschmann, and Paolo
    Perulli, (1993). "The Emergence of the Euro-company: Towards
    European Industrial Relations?" *Industrial Relations Journal*, vol. 24,
    182-189.

Marsden, David (1990). "Institutions and Labour Mobility: Occupational and
    Internal Labour Markets in Britain, France, Italy and West Germany."
    In Renato Brunetta and Carlo Dell'Aringa, eds., *Labour Relations and
    Economic Performance*. London: Macmillan, 414-438.

Maurice, M., F. Seller, and J-J. Silvestre (1986). *The Social Foundations of
    Industrial Power: A Comparison of France and Germany*. Cambridge
    Mass: MIT Press.

Michels, Ank, and Hans Slomp (1990). "The Role of Government in
    Collective Bargaining: Scandinavia and the Low Countries."
    Scandinavian Political Studies, vol. 13, 21-35.

Michie, Jonathan, and John Grieve Smith, eds. (1994). *Unemployment in
    Europe*. London: Academic Press.

Moerel, Hans (ed). (1994). *Labour Relations in Transition*. Nijmegen: ITS.

Moses, Jonathan W. (1993). "Abdication from National Policy Autonomy:
    What's Left to Leave." *Politics and Society*, vol. 22, 125-148.

Mueller, Frank, and John Purcell (1992). "The Europeanization of
    Manufacturing and the Decentralization of Bargaining: Multinational
    Management Strategies in the European Automobile Industry."
    International Journal of Human Resource Management, vol. 3, 15-34.

Mueller, Wolfgang C., and Vincent Wright (1994). "Reshaping the State in
    Western Europe: The Limits to Retreat." *West European Politics*, vol.
    17, no. 3, 1-11.

Nagelkerke, Ad (1995). "European Social Policy and European Industrial
    Relations." In Anne-Wil Harzing and Joris Van Ruysseveldt, eds.,
    International Human Resource Management: An Integrated Approach.
    London: Sage, 337-362.

Notermans, Ton (1993). "The Abdication from National Policy Autonomy:
    Why the Macroeconomic Policy Regime Has become So Unfavorable

to Labor." *Politics and Society*, vol. 21, 133-167.

Olson, Mancur (1965). *The Logic of Collective Action: Public Goods and the Theory of Groups*. Cambridge MA: Harvard University Press.

Ozaki, Muneto, (1992). *Technological Change and Labour Relations*. Geneva: International Labor Organization.*

Padgett, Stephen, and William E. Paterson (1991). *A History of Social Democracy in Postwar Europe*. London: Longman.

Paloheimo, Heikki (1990). Between Liberalism and Corporatism: The Effect of Trade Unions and Governments on Economic Performance in Eighteen OECD Countries. In Renato Brunetta and Carlo Dell'Aringa, eds., *Labour Relations and Economic Performance*. London: Macmillan, 114-136.

Paterson, William E. and A.H. Thomas, eds. (1986). *The Future of Social Democracy: Problems and Prospects of Social Democratic Parties in Western Europe*. Oxford: Clarendon Press.

Pekkarinen, J., M. Pohjola, and B. Rowthorn (1991). "Social Corporatism and Economic Performance." In J. Pekkarinen, M. Pohjola, B. Rowthorn, eds., *Social Corporatism*. Oxford: Clarendon Press, 1-23.

Pontusson, Jonas (1992). "Unions, New Technology, and Job Redesign at Volvo and British Leyland." In Miriam Golden and Jonas Pontusson, eds., *Bargaining for Change: Union Politics in North America and Europe*. Ithaca NY: Cornell University Press, 277-306.

Pontusson, Jonas, and S. Kuruvilla (1992). "Swedish Wage-Earner Funds: An Experiment in Economic Democracy." *Industrial and Labor Relations Review*, vol. 45, 779-791.

Przeworski, Adam (1985). *Capitalism and Social Democracy*. Cambridge: Cambridge University Press.

Regini, Mario ed. (1992). *The Future of Labour Movements*. London: Sage.

- - - (1993). "Human Resource Management and Industrial Relations in European Companies." *International Journal of Human Resource Management*, vol. 4, 555-568.

Rhodes, Martin (1991). "The Social Dimension of the Single European

Market: National Versus Transnational Regulation." *European Journal of Political Research*, vol. 19, 245-280.

- - - (1992). "The Future of the 'Social Dimension': Labour Market Regulation in Post-1992 Europe." *Journal of Common Market Studies*, vol. 30, 23-51.

Rimlinger, Gaston V. (1971). *Welfare Policy and Industrialization in Europe, America and Russia*. New York: Wiley.

Rubery, Jill (1992). "Pay, Gender and the Social Dimension to Europe." *British Journal of Industrial Relations*, vol. 30, 605-621.

Rubery, Jill and Colette Fagan (1994). "Does Feminization Mean a Flexible Labour Force?" In Richard Hyman and Anthony Ferner, eds., *New Frontiers in European Industrial Relations*. Oxford: Basil Blackwell, 140-166.

Scharpf, Fritz (1990). *Crisis and Choice in European Social Democracy*. Ithaca NY: Cornell University Press.

Schmitter, Philippe C. (1974). "Still the Century of Corporatism." *The Review of Politics*, vol. 36, 85-131.

Schmitter, Philippe C., and Gerhard Lehmbruch, eds. (1979). *Trends Toward Corporatist Intermediation*. London: Sage.

Schmitter, Philippe C., and Wolfgang Streeck (1991). "From National Corporatism to Transnational Pluralism: Organized Interests in the Single European Market." *Politics and Society*, vol. 19, no. 2, 133-164.

Scholten, I. (ed). (1987). *Political Stability and Neo-Corporatism*. London: Sage.

Shalev, M. (1992). "The Resurgence of Labour Quiescence." In Marino Regini, ed., *The Future of Labour Movements*. London: Sage, 102-132.

Shorter, Edward, and Charles Tilly (1974). *Strikes in France 1830-1968*. New York: Cambridge University Press.

Sisson, Keith (1987). *The Management of Collective Bargaining: An International Comparison*. Oxford: Basil Blackwell.

Slomp, Hans (1990). *Labor Relations in Europe: A History of Issues and*

Developments. Westport CT: Greenwood Press.

- - - (1992). "European Labor Relations and the Prospects of Tripartism." In Tiziano Treu, ed., *Participation in Public Policy-Making: The Role of Trade Unions and Employers' Associations*. Berlin: Walter de Gruyter, 159-173.

- - - (1995). "National Variations in Worker Participation." In Anne-Wil Harzing and Joris Van Ruysseveldt, eds., *International Human Resource Management: An Integrated Approach*. London: Sage, 291-317.

Soskice, David (1990). "Reinterpreting Corporatism and Explaining Unemployment: Co-ordinated and Non-co-ordinated Market Economies." In Renato Brunetta and Carlo Dell'Aringa, eds., *Labour Relations and Economic Performance*. London: Macmillan, 170-209.

Streeck, Wolfgang (1984). *Industrial Relations in West Germany: A Case Study of the Car Industry*. London: Heinemann.

- - - (1992). *Social Institutions and Economic Performance: Studies of Industrial Relations in Advanced Capitalist Economies*. London: Sage.

Swenson, Peter (1985). *Fair Shares: Unions, Pay and Politics in Sweden and West Germany*. Ithaca NY: Cornell University Press.

- - - (1992). "Union Politics, the Welfare State, and Intraclass Conflict in Sweden and Germany." In Miriam Golden and Jonas Pontusson, eds., *Bargaining for Change: Union Politics in North America and Europe*. Ithaca NY: Cornell University Press, 45-76.

Taylor, Andrew J. (1993). "Trade Unions and the Politics of Social Democratic Renewal." *West European Politics*, vol. 16, 133-155.

Teague, Paul (1989). "European Community Labour Market Harmonisation." *Journal of Public Policy*. vol. 9, no. 1, 1-33.

- - - (1993). "Towards Social Europe? Industrial Relations after 1992." *International Journal of Human Resource Management*, vol. 4, 349-375.

Teague, Paul, and John Grahl (1992). *Industrial Relations and European Integration*. London: Lawrence and Wisehart.

Thelen, Kathleen (1992). *Union of Parts: Labor Relations in Post-War Germany*. Ithaca NY: Cornell University Press.

- - - (1993). "West European Labor in Transition: Sweden and Germany Compared." *World Politics*, vol. 46, 23-49.

Therborn, Göran (1986). *Why Some Peoples Are More Unemployed Than Others*. London: Verso.

- - - (1989). "'Pillarization' and 'Popular Movements': Two Variants of Welfare State Capitalism: the Netherlands and Sweden." In Francis G. Castles, ed., *The Comparative History of Public Policy*. Cambridge: Polity Press, 192-241.

- - - (1991). "Lessons from 'Corporatist' Theoratizations." In J. Pekkarinen, M. Pohjola, and B. Rowthorn, eds., *Social Corporatism*. Oxford: Clarendon Press, 24-43.

Tokunaga, Shigeyoshi, Norbert Altmann, and Helmut Demes, eds. (1992). *New Impacts on Industrial Relations: Internationalization and Changing Production Strategies*. Munich: Iudicium Verlag.

Treu, Tiziano, ed. (1987). *Public Service Labour Relations*. Geneva: International Labor Organization.

Turner, Lowell (1991). *Democracy at Work: Changing World Markets and the Future of Labor Unions*. Ithaca NY: Cornell University Press.

Uvalic, Milica (1993). "Workers' Financial Participation in the European Community." *Economic and Industrial Democracy*, vol. 14, 185-194.

Van Hoof, Jacques, Hans Slomp, and Kitty Verrips, eds. (1992). *Westbound? Changing Industrial Relations in Eastern Europe*. Amsterdam: Siswo.

Visser, Jelle (1990). *In Search of Inclusive Unionism*. Deventer: Kluwer.

- - - (1992). The Strength of Union Movements in Advanced Capitalist Democracies: Social and Organizational Variations. In Marino Regini, ed., *The Future of Labour Movements*. London: Sage, 17-52.

Windmuller, John P., and Alan Gladstone, eds. (1984). *Employer Associations and Industrial Relations: A Comparative Study*. Oxford: Oxford Univesity Press.

Windmuller, John P., (1987). *Collective Bargaining in Industrialised Market Economies: A Reappraisal*. Geneva: International Labor Organization.*

Index

Absenteeism, 110
Action directe, 9, 20, 36, 131
Affirmative action, 58, 122
Alpine Countries, *See* Austria, Switzerland
Americanization of labor relations, 147-148
Anarchism, 35-36
Auroux laws, 99-101, 123
Austria, xiii, 5-8, 42, 51, 68, 74-75, 79, 82, 85, 98, 132-134
Autogestion, 80
Autunno caldo, 11-12, 21, 42, 88

Basic Agreement, 6, 40, 128
BDA (*Bundesvereinigung deutscher Arbeitgeberverbände*), 22
Belgium, xiii, 1, 6-8, 11, 17, 34-35, 50, 68-69, 73-75, 81, 85-86, 94, 103, 130-132. *See also* Low Countries
Beveridge, William, 41, 111
Bismarck, Otto von, 37, 110-111
British model of labor relations, general nature and organizations, xiii-xv, 13-15, 61, 125-126, 141; and politics, 18-19, 21-26, 50; collective bargaining, 65-66, 84; worker participation, 80-84, labor conditions, 104

Bulgaria, xiv-xv, 56. *See also* Central Europe
Bullock Committee, 80

Castles, Francis, 23
Catholic Church, 3-4, 42, 47, 60, 121
Catholic organizations, 6-8, 16-19, 23, 35, 42, 119, 142
CBI (Confederation of British Industry), 22, 119
Central Europe, xiv, 39, 42-44, 55-57
Certification, 144
CGIL (*Confederazione Generale Italiana del Lavoro*), 20, 40
CGT (*Confédération générale du travail*), 11, 20, 36, 38, 40, 118, 120
Charter of Amiens, 36
Christian Democrats, 23-25, 49, 54, 111, 130-132. *See also* Catholic organizations
Clegg, Hugh, 64, 69
Clerical workers, 16, 46-49, 56, 76, 93, 105, 144
Closed shop, 14-16, 98, 146-147
CNPF (*Conseil national du patronat français*), 22
Co-determination, 79-80, 89-90

Cold War, 40, 80, 89
Collective bargaining, xi-xiv, 19,
  21, 26-28, 36, 41, 64-77, 119, 144-
  146
Communists, 10, 20-21, 38-39,
  42-44, 49, 53-55, 119, 135-139
Concession bargaining, 104
Confindustria, 23
Conservatives, 10, 19, 23, 26,
  49-50, 77, 98, 105, 143
Corporatism, 1-9, 12, 27, 60-61, 73,
  119, 127, 130, 133, 148
Craft unions, 13-18, 31, 37, 64-66,
  79, 94
Crouch, Colin, 61
Czechoslovakia, 43-44, 55-56. *See
  also* Central Europe

De Gaulle, Charles, 25, 106
Delors, Jacques, 118
Demarcation disputes, 15-16
Denmark, xiii, 6, 8, 17, 64, 72-74,
  81, 85, 113, 121, 127-130. *See
  also* Scandinavia
De-politicization, 3, 68-69
DGB (*Deutsche
  Gewerkschaftsbund*), 9-12, 16-17,
  19, 48, 82, 120, 124
Dilution, 14
Direct action, 9, 20, 36, 131
Donovan Commission, 65

Einheitsgewerkschaft, 16
Employer prerogative, 87
Employment policy, 39, 74, 98,
  112-114
Engineers, 32
Environmentalism, 57-59
Estatuto de los Trabajadores, 12,
  82
ETUC (European Trade Union
  Confederation), 119-122, 124

EU (European Union), 48, 80,
  109-110, 113, 115-126
European works council, 80,
  123-125

Fascism, 17, 25, 39-40, 55, 79, 135,
  143
Feminism, 42, 47, 58-59
Fiat, 39, 89, 97
Finland, xiv, 47, 97-98, 107-109
Flexi-time, 47, 97-98, 107-109
Fordism, 91, 96
France, xiii-xvi, 47, 77; central
  level, 5, 9-11; organizations, 17,
  20, 54; labor relations and politics,
  xiii, 24-25, 28-29, 38, 40;
  collective bargaining, 42, 69-71,
  99; worker participation, 54, 80-
  83, 87-89, 99-101, 109; labor
  conditions, 105-107, 113, 121, 124
French Revolution, 32, 142
Friendly societies, 14, 32, 110

General workers, 14, 37
Generalkommission, 34
Germanic model of labor relations,
  general nature and organizations,
  xiii-xv, 15-18, 34-42, 60-61, 125-
  126, 141, 145; and politics, 19-21,
  25-31, 49-53, 108; collective
  bargaining, 66-69, 77, 93-95, 98;
  worker participation, 85-90, 100;
  labor conditions, 112-114
Germany, xiii-xvi, 75; central level,
  9-12, 51, 74, 143; organizations, 9,
  17, 19, 48; labor relations and
  politics, 33-39, 49-50; collective
  bargaining, 42, 67-69, 72, 76, 93-
  98; worker participation, 79-90,
  93-97, 100; labor conditions, 105-
  108, 113, 118-119, 121
Gorbachev, Mikhail, 44

Great Britain, xiii-xvi, 31, 47; central level, 9-10; organizations, 9-10, 13-18, 22, 33, 37; labor relations and politics, 18-19, 22-27, 38, 50-51, 73, 109; collective bargaining, 65-66, 84, 94, 98, 104; worker participation, 80-84; labor conditions, 104, 107, 111-113, 117-118, 121-124
Great Strike, 26
Greece, xiv-xv, 21, 55
Grenelle, Constat de, 11, 28, 42, 83
Groupes d'expression, 101

Health and safety, 46, 83, 109, 121
Holidays, 46, 83, 108
Holland, 1, 6-7, 17, 23, 42, 61, 67-69, 74, 82, 85, 97, 113, 118, 130-132. *See also* Low Countries
Hot Autumn, 11-12, 21, 42, 88
Hovedaftale, 6
Human Resources Management, 101
Hungary, xiv-xv, 43-44, 56, 137-139. *See also* Central Europe

Iberian Peninsula, 24-25, 54-55, 99. *See also* Portugal, Spain
IG Metall (*Industriegewerkschaft Metall*), 48, 67, 90, 98, 100, 107, 126
ILO (International Labor Organization), 39, 122
Immigrants, 47, 58-59, 117
Industrial unions, 15-18
Inflation, 42, 45
Ireland, xiii-xiv, 66, 73, 104, 109
Italy xiii-xv; central level, 9-12, 70, 88-89; organizations, 9-10, 17, 20-21, 61; labor relations and politics, 4, 23-25, 35, 38, 40, 55; collective bargaining, 70-71, 75, 97; worker participation, 88-89; labor conditions, 103-105

Japan, 45-46, 100, 110

Katzenstein, Peter J., 5, 8
Keynes, John Maynard, 40
Keynesianism, 40-42, 50-52
Konzertierte Aktion, 10, 74
Korpi, Walter, 7-8

Labor legislation, 26-29, 39, 68-71, 98, 114
Labor peace, 35, 40, 64-68, 71
Labour Party, 10, 18, 21, 26, 37, 49, 74, 118
Latin model of labor relations, general nature and organizations, xiii-xv, 15-18, 35-42, 53-55, 61, 126, 141-142; and politics, 20-21, 24, 28-29, 34-39, 49-50, 53, 108; collective bargaining, 69-71, 77, 94, 99; worker participation, 87-89, 94; labor conditions, 112-114
Lenin, Vladimir, 20, 38, 43
Liberal-labor cooperation, 18, 32, 37-38
Liberals, 23, 32, 37, 49
Locke, Richard, 97
Lockout, 15, 32, 68
Low Countries, 2, 5-9, 16-19, 42, 95, 98, 113. *See also* Belgium, Holland
Luebbert, Gregory M., 38

Maastricht Treaty, 117
Matignon, 11, 21, 28, 40, 79
MBL (*Medbestämmandelagen*), 80, 92, 93
Meidner Proposal, 92-93
Metallurgy, 31, 40, 48, 67, 72
Minimum wage, 104-106
Mining, 26, 31, 33, 41-42, 109

Mitbestimmung, 89-90
Morocco, 47-48, 59

National Front, 40
Nationalization, 40, 75, 89
Nazism, 17, 25, 39-40, 79
Norway, xiii, 6, 8, 40, 72, 113,
  127-130. *See also* Scandinavia

Oil crisis, 42, 45-46, 50, 57, 73
Old-age pensions, 108-111
Olson, Mancur, 22

Pacification of labor relations,
  64-65, 86-87
Paris Commune, 34
Parliamentary democracy, 5, 34-38
Pattern bargaining, 67, 126
Poland, xiv-xv, 43-44, 55-57,
  137-139. *See also* Central Europe
Political levy, 18-19
Political strike, 20, 26, 28, 35
Popular Front, 39-40
Portugal, xiii, 17, 20, 24-25, 43-44,
  54-57, 70, 99, 114, 135-136
Positive action, 58, 122
Printing industry, 33-36, 43
Profit sharing, 106
Protestantism, 8, 19, 23, 35. *See
  also* Christian Democrats
Public sector, 23, 42, 49, 52-54, 59,
  70, 75-77, 113

Quality circles, 100

Railways, 33, 36, 53
Renault, 75
Russia, 39-44
Russian Revolution, 38-39, 43, 111

Saltsjöbaden Agreement, 6, 40
Scandinavia, xiv, 2, 5-9, 24-28,
  34-35, 66, 68, 81, 98, 111-112,
  128. *See also* Denmark, Norway,
  Sweden
Schmitter, Philippe, 3-4
SDAP (*Sozialdemokratische
  Arbeiterpartei*), 33
Septemberforlig, 64
Sexual harassment, 110
Sisson, Keith, 64
Sociaal-Economische Raad, 1-2,
  130-132
Social Charter, 117-119
Social Contract, 10, 74
Social democrats, 7-10, 18-22,
  25-28, 33-38, 45, 49-52, 59, 92,
  111, 118, 129
Social legislation, 26-29, 37, 39, 57,
  68-71, 98, 114
Social Pact, 6
Social peace, 35, 40, 64, 66-68, 71
Social security, 37, 41, 110-112,
  122, 147-148
Socialists, 21, 54
Solidaristic wage policy, 72, 91-94
Solidarność, 44, 55, 137-138
Soviet Union, xiv
Spain, xiii, 20-21, 24-25, 35, 40,
  54-55, 71, 82, 88, 99, 114, 135-
  136
Spontaneous action, 9, 20, 36, 131
Statuto dei Lavoratori, 12
Steel industry, 31, 41, 46
Streeck, Wolfgang, 94-95
Sudreau Committee, 80
Sweden, xiii, 5-8, 17, 40, 42, 48-51,
  72-74, 77, 80-81, 85-87, 91-96,
  113. *See also* Scandinavia
Swenson, Peter, 72
Switzerland, xiii, 5-8, 17-19, 40,
  59, 61, 67-68, 74, 113, 132-134

Tarifautonomie, 74
Textile industry, 16, 32-33, 46, 97
TGWU (Transport and General
  Workers Union), 14
Thatcher, Margaret, 50-51, 117
Therborn, Göran, 113
Trade Union Act, 19
Training, 93-96, 107, 113
Transmission belt, 20, 43
Tripartism, 1-4, 9-12, 55-57, 99,
  136-138
TUC (Trade Union Congress), 9-10,
  15, 18, 32-33, 37, 120, 124, 137
Turkey, 47, 59

Unemployment, 45, 50-51, 57, 91,
  98, 112-116
UNICE (Union of Industrial and
  Employers' Confederations in
  Europe), 120-123
Unified unionism, 16
Unionization rate, 17, 48, 60, 91
United States, xv, 58-61, 141-148

Visser, Jelle, 17
Volkswagen, 67-68, 107, 124
Voting rights, 34, 58

Wage Councils, 65, 105
Wage differentials, 101-107, 117
Wage earner funds, 92-93, 106
Wage indexation, 75, 103
Wage policy, 3, 73-77
Welfare state, 41, 46, 92, 110-114,
  147-148
Women, 47-48, 58-59, 98, 106,
  110, 122
Worker participation, xii-xiv, 79-90,
  92-95, 123-125, 146-147
Workers' councils, 43
Workers' Statute, 12, 82
Working time, 107-109, 122
Works council, 80-89
World War, First, 31, 38, 42, 64,
  79, 88, 111, 142; Second, 6, 11,
  17, 25, 31, 40, 43, 75, 142

Yellow unionism, 39

About the Author

HANS SLOMP is Lecturer in the Department of Political Science at the Catholic University of Nijmegen in the Netherlands. He is the author of *Labor Relations in Europe: A History of Issues and Developments* (Greenwood, 1990).

ISBN 0-275-95608-3

HARDCOVER BAR CODE